How to Succeed In Contracting By Really Trying

How to Succeed In Contracting By Really Trying

Six Steps to Success in Heating, Air Conditioning, Mechanical Contracting, and HVAC Service

(OR ANY OTHER BUSINESS)

William R Chandler

Any resemblance to actual persons, living or dead, events, or locales is entirely coincidental and are strictly products of the authors imagination.

Disclaimer: The author of this book is not liable for any damages or loses associated with the content or references. You must do your own research to determine what's best for you. You are responsible for your own life and/or business decisions and actions.

ISBN-10: 1523730706
ISBN-13: 978-1523730704

10 9 8 7 6 5 4 3 2 1

CONTENTS

CONTENTS

6S = CS

Dedication:

I would like to dedicate this book to my wife, Beth, who has always loved and supported me throughout my career and my life, no matter what.

Every time I came home and told her I wanted to try something new in my career and we ended up moving, she was always supportive of the change in our lives and encouraged me every step of the way.

In the construction industry, you don't always get to choose where you live. But with her in my life, each destination was always home.

Whenever we moved to a new home, the first item we set out was a framed verse, written by Henry Van Dyke, that we purchased early on in our marriage for our very first house. It always made us feel as though we were home, no matter where we were. It says the following:

"Every house where love abides
And friendship is a guest,
Is surely home sweet home
For there the heart can rest."

My wife has been my best friend and my confidant, and she has encouraged and supported me throughout our life together.

When I'm with her, I'm always at home and my heart can always rest.

Introduction and About the Author:

In the crazy world of business, whether it's the PHVACR (plumbing, heating, ventilating, air conditioning, and refrigeration) service, mechanical contracting, or really any other business, we all go to work and do our best and hope that we succeed.

I've worked in and consulted for a number of PHVACR companies in my lifetime, and the one thing that always struck me was that most of these businesses never really had a solid plan in place to get to where they wanted to go. In fact, most of them really didn't know where they were going. That's where this book comes in.

They were all going through the motions and enjoying the rewards, when there were some, and feeling the pain when things went bad.

I watched how the owners struggled with the day-to-day running of their businesses and how they always seemed to revert back to the way their mothers, fathers, uncles, grandfathers, or previous owners had run the operations, and this never really delivered the results that they wanted.

As I grew more confident in my positions with these firms, I began to speak up and ask the hard questions that most of the owners couldn't answer. This usually led to their becoming somewhat annoyed by the types of questions that were being asked.

I tried staying quiet at one of the firms, and this drove me crazy. I became one of those dutiful go-along employees. You know who they are. They show up every day, keep their heads down, try not to be noticed, and just do their jobs.

My guess is that some of your employees are like this, and that's OK. But you need to make sure you also have some people who push you to do better and who are not afraid to ask the hard and uncomfortable questions. Just try not to get annoyed at them.

Simply put, you need some people who will support down and challenge up.

If you don't have anyone like this, then this book can act as a substitute and ask you those tough questions that need to be asked. This book is for those individuals who are ready to try something new.

In fact, the ideas I share in this book are not really new. They are basic business 101 principles, but as I've discovered, most owners have forgotten many of these basics. This book is for those leaders who understand what leadership is truly about, not the micromanagers (you know who you are), unless you're ready for a change.

If you're looking to improve your operations, your leadership skills, your ability to have more fun and enjoy coming to work as you did when you first started, then this book is for you.

If you are looking for a way to improve your current operations so you can either sell your business or get it ready to pass on to the next generation, then this book can help. Also, if you're thinking about starting a business or if your current business is still young, then you definitely want to continue reading this book.

I remember going to association meetings and starting conversations about basic business concepts and what I've learned during my career. I was often astonished to hear comments like, "You should write a book" or "I could listen to you talk all day." I was surprised because all this seemed to me to be normal day-to-day business. (In reality, I could have listened to them all day, too, since I learned some of my best lessons in life at these meetings.)

As it turned out, the information I was sharing during these conversations may have seemed routine to me, but it wasn't routine to many of the others, and they really wanted to hear more.

That's what led me to write about what I have learned in my life and what I hope will be a reminder that even though we think we know what we're doing, we can always use a little help.

I know most of you have never heard of William R Chandler and are wondering why in the world you should spend your hard-earned money on his book.

Well, the choice is yours. However, I learned a long time ago that all people can teach you something, whether they are young or old, a CEO or someone you meet on the street.

It's just a matter of keeping an open mind and finding something in the conversation (or book) that will teach you a lesson on either *what to do*, or *what not to do.*

See, it's just that simple.

In this book, I often mention how I learned *what not to do* in business by observing the things owners, utilities, and consolidators did that just didn't work.

By *just didn't work,* I mean they never delivered the results that they could have, had more thought been put into them. (Really Trying!)

Also, I learned about *what not to do* by making lots of mistakes in my life. On the flip side, along the way I discovered things *to do* that really did work. Many are included in my six-step program.

I was born on an Army base in the Northwest (yes, I'm an Army brat) and was raised in southern California. Even as young boys, my older brother, Ray, and I worked in my dad's auto garage/junkyard.

I always hated working in the garage because I wanted to be playing with my friends after school and during the summer holidays. But I never could.

Time went by, and when I was thirteen, the family moved back to northern Indiana where my mom and dad were born and raised. But my brother and I still had to work in the new auto garage/junkyard my dad opened in Indiana.

I decided early in life that I really didn't like this type of work. It was too dirty and too hard! At the time, I didn't realize that *all* of life is hard work, and that's just the way it is.

Introduction and About the Author

My dad died of a tragic accident in our garage when I was barely sixteen years old. Since my brother and sister had already left home, my mom and I had to figure out what to do next. My mom had a severe health condition, so it was really up to me.

Dad didn't have much insurance, and we had no assets except the junk cars my dad had acquired, which were sitting in the yard.

I remember the funeral home wanted payment no later than the morning of my dad's funeral, and we needed to raise additional money in order to bury my father.

I went out into the junkyard by myself on the morning of my dad's funeral and decided that I could cut up car frames, load the frames onto a trailer, drive my dad's eighteen-wheeler on the back roads to Kokomo, Indiana to the metal scrapyard, and sell them to raise the money we needed.

It had rained the night before, and the ground was muddy. At first light, I put my boots on and went to the yard to start lifting cars on their side with a hook from our boom truck, so I could cut the frames off the car bodies.

I had cut and stacked enough scrap metal for a full load, but decided I had room for one more frame. I lifted the last car on its side and started cutting, but all of a sudden, the hook holding it up came loose, and the entire car frame fell on top of me.

I was pinned under the frame and couldn't move. The mud had helped absorb some of the crush of the car frame, but I was having trouble breathing, and no one was around to help me.

I was lying there thinking about how my mother would kill me for this, when it hit me that she probably wouldn't need to kill me since I would already be dead if I couldn't get the car off me in the next few minutes.

They say your life flashes before you when you are facing death, and I'm here to tell you that it's true.

At the time, I wished that I had been much older than sixteen, since it only took about ten seconds for my entire life to go by, and I was still facing death. I decided then and there I was not going to die, miss my father's funeral and cause my poor mother more pain and grief.

So, I closed my eyes, said a quick prayer and pushed as hard as I could with my one-hundred-and-forty-pound body. Miraculously, as if someone else were doing the lifting for me, I was able to raise this heavy car frame enough to slide myself out from under it and let it drop.

I sat there for a minute, exhausted and trying to catch my breath, when it hit me. I had just lifted a car frame? That's impossible!

To this day, I believe that someone else was there with me, and that my prayers were truly answered.

The only permanent damage to me was a broken blood vessel on my lower lip that pushed itself to the surface (from all the straining). I looked as though someone had hit me in the mouth.

Well, I recovered, loaded the last car frame, drove the semi on the back roads of Indiana all the way down to Kokomo, and returned home. I was able to get cleaned up and to my father's funeral in time to pay the additional money we owed the funeral home, without my mother ever knowing what had happened that morning.

I never told my mother about my actions that day, and I still have the bulging blood vessel on my lip. Each day of my life, when I look into a mirror and see my lip, I'm reminded that we all can do *anything* we put our minds to, as long as we believe in ourselves, and never fear failure.

In the back of my mind, I always thought that maybe my dad had something to do with that car falling on me that morning. Maybe it was that last lesson my father wanted to teach me about having faith and believing that I could accomplish anything if I put my mind to it. He just didn't have the chance to teach me before he died.

After graduating from high school, I went to work in a tool and die department as a draftsman.

Then I had the opportunity to work for two architectural/engineering firms, first in Indiana and then in Ohio. Through these experiences, I learned that many great people worked in our industry.

The engineers for whom I worked took the time to teach me engineering skills through on-the-job training. They would also lend me their college books to study, test me on the content, and give me opportunities to apply it.

After a few years, I was engineering projects on my own, and they would stamp the drawings after they reviewed my designs.

When the recession hit, I was laid off. Fortunately, I was given the opportunity to work for the PHVACR firm that had been the low bidder on the final two jobs I had just engineered.

WOW, what an eye opener!

I thought I knew everything about construction, having spent the last six years of my life designing projects and pointing out to contractors through the dreaded punch list, what they needed to correct.

I quickly discovered that I knew very little about the construction industry. The first time I went to the construction site of one of the schools I had just engineered, I tried to tell the pipefitting foreman that he was not installing the pipe the way I had designed it. His reaction was not what I had expected.

He grabbed me by the back of my coat, lifted me off my feet, took me to the edge of the building (which was about four feet above the ground) and threw me off!

Then he said, “Don’t ever come onto my jobsite again and tell me what to do!”

Wow, what a life changing lesson that was!

That day I learned the importance of effective communication. People in the construction industry, and I’m certain in any industry, take a great deal of pride in what they do. They don’t appreciate anyone telling them what or how to do it.

All people want to be respected, no matter what they do for a living, and approaching them with this in mind will help support a win-win result if you're trying to offer constructive suggestions.

Remember, you must first give respect before you can get respect.

If you stop reading this book right now and follow just this one lesson, I promise that you will get your money back many times over.

As my career progressed, I worked for larger and larger PHVACR mechanical contractors as a project engineer, senior project manager, treasurer, general manager, director of sales and marketing, regional manager, vice president, member of a board of directors, COO, partner, CEO/president and owner.

I've worked for architectural/engineering firms and PHVACR mechanical contractors with annual volumes as large as $500 million.

I've also worked with utility companies during the consolidation era doing $8 billion in revenue. Additionally, I've worked with mechanical contracting and service national consolidators having 250 plus companies nationwide, that produced $600 million in revenue annually.

Along the way, I've managed and consulted with PHVACR service departments, energy management and consulting divisions, sheet metal shops, pipe fabrication shops, fire protection divisions, underground utility divisions, and mechanical contracting firms. I've also managed sales and marketing divisions for our industry.

Through all these experiences, I learned that by implementing certain processes, I was able to produce a successful product and provide great service.

Over time, this became my formula or 'six steps to success' program, which I've shared with anyone who wanted to listen. I often heard people suggest that I write a book, and that led me to where I am today.

I hope you enjoy this book and, at the very minimum, come away with at least one idea to make your business or your life better. If that idea works, share it with someone else, and help our industry continue to be more professional.

Thanks to everyone who helped and supported me throughout my career and contributed to my success. I will always be grateful for the life lessons you helped me learn.

You never fully know the impact you've had on people. Did you contribute in some way to their success… or failure?

It's not about what I've done or what positions I've held during my career. It's always been about the journey. Don't forget to stop along the way and reflect on where you've been and dream about where you would like to go. Once you get to where you're going, turn around and help those behind you.

Please remember while reading this book that I'm not trying to tell anyone how to run their business or their life. I'm simply sharing what worked for me during my career. Try to pay attention to the lessons I've learned and to my success formula, then apply what works for you while integrating your own ideas and those of your employees.

Think about what goals you would like to accomplish and then set the strategy in motion to reach them.

You, too, can make a difference!

6S = CS

$6S = CS$

Chapter One
Step One - A New Beginning

A New Beginning. I mean that literally!

It's time to sit down and reevaluate your business, which is the real description of what *A New Beginning* is. Where are you? Where have you been? Where are you going? Step one is that proverbial "each journey begins with taking the first step" phase.

There are six steps in this book, but this is the biggest step you'll need to take. I promise you that once you've completed taking this first big step, you'll be able to decide if you're ready (or even want) to take the next five.

Let's jump right in and get started, shall we?

Throughout my career, I needed to develop and write various marketing plans for businesses I knew something about. Initially, my major problem was that I had never written a business/marketing plan, nor did I have a clue about where to start.

That put me on a journey of researching and learning, and I was finally able to put together what turned out to be the ghost of *A New Beginning - Past.*

If this sounds a little like Scrooge,
you might be right.

I was in the 'bah humbug' mood when I started the research because I just didn't see the need to do all that work when the businesses were doing - what I thought at the time - just fine. (Sound familiar?)

As my career advanced, so did the sophistication of my approach to managing different divisions of the PHVACR industry (e.g., mechanical contracting, fire protection, sheet metal, special projects, energy management, plumbing, PHVACR service, consulting, etc.).

Yes, these 'steps' work for all the above (and any other business) if you modify some of the ideas. I always felt that the service sector offered the most opportunity for mechanical contractors to build a foundation that would help support the organization in good times and down times.

But I'm certain none of you have ever experienced down times in the PHVACR construction industry, right? (Yah, right!)

As time went on and I learned more and more about the industry, I grew to appreciate the sophistication of what it really takes to be successful.

I had the privilege to be involved with the utility consolidation and the purchasing of mechanical contracting and service companies at the time of de-regulation. Companies believed they could bundle their services and continue to retain their current customer base, while developing new customers. Many failed miserably and eventually sold the acquired companies back to the original owners.

Believe me, I don't recall a single owner who didn't want to buy back their business.

I believe that most (not all) business owners are *entrepreneurs* and really struggle to work for someone else, no matter how hard they try or how strongly they believe they can.

It was during this time that I had the opportunity to talk to my peers about their businesses. I learned the differences between the owners and how each ran his or her particular business and approached the day-to-day operations within the various markets. It became clear that most business owners were running their businesses just as their uncles, mothers, fathers or grandfathers had run them for years. After all, they had been successful, right?

This follows the old 'if it isn't broken, don't fix it' belief, which might have worked in the past, but not in today's market.

That led me to do more research and adjust my original thoughts on the need for business/marketing plans. It started to make sense that having a solid plan was really necessary if I wanted to succeed in helping others change their business philosophy and culture.

After my exposure to the utility consolidation period, I was lucky enough to enter the mechanical contracting, service company consolidation and roll-up phase of the PHVACR industry. At the time, it seemed this was the wave of the future.

If you wanted your company to survive, you had better consider either selling your firm or joining one of those 'Masters of the Industry' companies that promised to help you grow your business, give you access to a network of other contractors, and provide support in accounting, legal, purchasing, national branding, best practices, marketing, etc.

This experience allowed me to work with different business owners and to observe which processes worked for each of them and which didn't. These companies were all operating in ways that the owners believed were just fine at the time, and the owners were all comfortable with the results.

I learned a great deal about the industry from the owners and how we are all linked, regardless of the areas of the country in which our businesses are operating.

We all deal with the same problems daily and ask ourselves the same questions. My time spent during this phase of our industry was enlightening and educational.

Within two or three years, most of the consolidators were purchased again and rolled into larger corporations. They hoped they knew more than the first consolidators knew and believed they could be successful.

In the end, however, many of them lost a bundle, laid off a large number of good people, sold back many of the businesses to the original owners (sound familiar?) and eventually either retained only a fraction of the original companies or went out of business altogether. I'm only telling you all this because it led me to develop what I believe to be this 'cookbook' for success.

Have you ever heard anyone say,
through adversity comes greatness?

I'm not sure it develops greatness, but it sure does keep you humble. I tell anyone who will listen that I may not always know what to do to fix your business, but I certainly know what *NOT* to do.

So, what's on the 'not to do' list?

First and foremost, doing *nothing* is on this list. Or worse, you should not do anything that's ineffective or counter to your strengths. This step is so critical because it forces you to honestly evaluate your business – what's working, what's not working, and what needs to change.

There's another saying that suggests, *if you continue to do what you've always done, you'll continue to get what you've always gotten.* If that's your pleasure, then please stop reading this book and pass it on to someone who truly is looking for *A New Beginning.*

But if you're ready for honest assessment and change, then please continue reading....

To get started, I would suggest you find someone you trust to oversee your business (with your remote input) while you get away to spend time evaluating your company - where you are, where you've been, and where you would like to take your business.

Do this after you've finished reading this book, not before.

If you're now telling yourself that this guy's nuts, and there's no way you can leave your business in someone else's hands to take time to evaluate your company's performance, then you really *DO* need to make this happen as soon as possible.

If not, you risk being stuck ten years from now in the same place that you are today, and you'll wonder where your life went and why you are married to your company instead of your partner.

Your family will have grown up and out of the house, and you'll be asking yourself where did the time go and why didn't you listen to that 'nut guy' ten years ago when he suggested you get away.

Well, now's your chance to *make a difference* in both your company and your life.

Here's what you'll need to do:

1) Gather copies of your financial statements from the last five years. If you don't have five years, take what you have.

2) Talk to your employees and gather their input on how to improve your business and make it better. Encourage each person to include at least one new idea.

3) Have a *minimum* of two or three copies of this book. Again, don't start this process until you've finished reading this book.

4) Gather as much information as possible about your competitors (the very best firms only). Some examples of information to include are rate per hour they currently charge, number of trucks they have, and all services they offer.

   What differentiates them from all the other companies in your market? What is their best product or service? Investigate where and how often they advertise, and who they use.

5) Have available the contact information for your accountant, banker, bonding company, advertising company, peer group members, and vendors you partner with the most.

6) Secure customer analytics from the last three years. This would be a list of customers showing total revenue, gross margin, and net profit for each.

7) Gather all the equipment and materials you'll need to capture and organize your thoughts and ideas (e.g., a good laptop computer, lots of easels and paper, markers, and some tape for hanging ideas on the walls) and bring a

few stress balls to throw around. (Maybe lots of stress balls would be better.)

Remember, no idea is bad, no matter how it sounds. Don't just think outside the box. Create a new type of box or cylinder or sphere. Really stretch your imagination.

8) Include anything else you can think of that will help you forge *A New Beginning.*

   Consider including your spouse or partner and family in this process. If possible and appropriate, ask them to participate and provide input. If you must be away from your family, be sure to stay in touch.

   Keep them updated on your progress. (Just in case you end up being away from home longer than you expected, you might want to have the phone number of a good florist, too.)

9) And last but not least, bring an open mind. This will be the toughest thing to pack, but it is the most important. You've probably been told many times that you can't change a leopard's spots, but I'm here to tell you that if the leopard can open his or her mind, those spots can change.

I've helped many business owners open their eyes to new ideas, and in return, we witnessed the spots change right before our eyes.

Now that you have everything you need, choose a location that will allow you to work and relax at the same time with as little distraction as possible.

Using a resort type location will allow you to work a little, then get away from it for a short time and come back refreshed from your walk or time spent in the spa or on the driving range, fishing or whatever relaxes you.

Taking breaks will give your mind time to unwind, and as it does, new ideas will start to float around that would have never occurred to you previously. Write them down, even if they sound weird or outrageous at the time. You just never know if or when you might want to reconsider an idea.

If it makes you more comfortable to ask for other people from your staff to join you, then by all means, do so. This will allow them to be a part of the solution to making your firm the best it can be, and they will feel more appreciated.

If you're not sure it's a good idea to have them with you the first few days, go by yourself. Prepare an outline first, then bring them in.

Before starting, make sure you have a plan for how to facilitate the meeting. If you're not sure, you can always hire a consultant to help you work through not only this initial phase but also all the phases. Whatever makes you most comfortable will also help you be more effective.

Completing this step doesn't have to happen overnight. In fact, it won't. It has always taken me a minimum of ninety days to perform a complete evaluation of a firm and to put together a new business strategy and marketing plan.

Keep in mind it could take a number of days, working long hours to get it right.

At the end of a long day, when you're feeling really tired and looking forward to a good meal, you'll find that some of your best ideas might start to flow, so don't cave too soon.

As you start this journey, please keep in mind that there are a million or more ways to look at a business.

Especially a contracting business!

This book assumes you already know about financial statements, margins, markup, how to price products you sell, rate per hour calculations, overhead calculations, and other related topics.

If you don't understand these and other basic terms or if you need help with any of them, then find resources that can help you. There are many professional organizations that offer their members education and advice on each of these subjects.

Participating in an industry peer group can also help you expand your knowledge. And don't forget all the great books, articles, and workshops that are available on these subjects.

Understanding these basic business terms and concepts are fundamental, and I will refer to many of them throughout this book.

Again, as I move you through these steps, I will focus on the basics of what you really need to be doing and thinking about to make your business successful going forward.

After meeting and talking with many business owners, I've discovered that they often don't have a plan to get them from point A to point B.

They just show up every day and go through the motions of running a business. They never take the time to ask themselves basic questions, such as What should they do next? or How will they meet their goals? and then search for the answers.

By now, I'm sure you're wondering about the meaning of the formula you've been seeing throughout this book.

This book will help you implement my basic philosophy (formula) of:

6s = Cs

(Or)

*Six **(6)** Steps **(s)** which also includes:*
Quality of the process +
Quality of the product +
Experience of the sale = Cs (or)

"Contracting (C) Success (s)"

I'll explain each of the components in detail as we move through the chapters.

Every morning when you arrive at work and unlock the door, do you know how much it's going to cost to run your business that day? Do you know how much revenue you need to generate to cover your overhead, how much gross margin you're expecting to make, or how much net profit you will need to generate?

By knowing this information, you can confidently and professionally make intelligent decisions throughout the day about the jobs you want to consider going after and how to structure the bids to get the margins you need. Knowing your business financial needs and goals on a daily basis will minimize surprises at the end of the month, quarter, or year. You'll know how or where the numbers should be.

In addition to knowing the numbers, you must constantly be aware of your target market and what you need to do to capture it. Also, you must totally understand your staff and know their capabilities, and they must be aligned with your company goals, mission, vision and culture.

After having implemented the *Quality of the process + Quality of the product + Experience of the sale* and the *Six Steps to Success* culture into multiple organizations, I'm confident that it will work for you.

Can you honestly say the same about how you are running your business today?

Now ask yourself if you really know what it takes not only to run your business, but also to successfully grow it and have fun doing it?

No doubt, many of you learned the basics of how to run a contracting business from your mother, dad, uncle or grandfather or by working for another contracting firm. You've gained solid experience working in the industry.

But despite this experience, do you sometimes feel that you're operating on auto-pilot and *hoping*, rather than *knowing*, that things will turn out at the end of the month or quarter or year. Do you really have it all figured out?

I'm sure you've heard the old phrase, 'hope is not a strategy.' Believe me, it's not.

I'll be attempting to lay out the basic processes I've used to help organizations turn themselves around. Along the way, I'll share some of my personal experiences with each step.

Through watching, listening, and learning from my peers and making lots of mistakes (remember, mistakes teach you *what not to do*), I've learned that the PHVACR business is a great business in which to work. But it's filled with challenges.

I believe that contractors are born optimists and believe they can overcome anything. In fact, they often can. But like all business owners, they need direction and feedback.

Many owners feel pressure every day when they go to work and struggle to just get through it. Other owners go into work happy and enjoy the day, but still don't really know where they are headed.

All companies tend to bid jobs that they should not be bidding, but they do it anyway because they're optimists. Most of the time, they lose the job, get depressed, then question how the other bidder could possibly have been that low?

Again, when you implement the *Quality of the process* + *Quality of the product* + *Experience of the sale* and *Six Steps to Success* philosophy into your organization, you will discover ways to eliminate these ups and downs, enjoy your days at work, and develop happier employees who are engaged in the process.

Let me give you just one example of *Quality of the process* to show you what I mean.

Let's start with a mechanical contracting firm, and let's say their closure rate for bids is around ten percent +/-. (A good closure rate should be around eighteen percent +/-).

This means that the company is awarded just one out of every ten jobs they bid. Believe it or not, that's not far off from the norm in our industry.

Talk about a waste of time and energy, not to mention the emotional ups and downs experienced by not only the owner, but also the estimators and everyone else in this firm when they repeatedly see the company lose that one big job they need to keep everyone working.

Wow! That's the steepest roller coaster there is. Just ask your employees. They'll tell you.

Let's now suppose this is your company. What can you do to change the scenario so that the company is in charge of the situation? Let's start by taking actions that support our *Quality of the process* commitment.

Below, I've listed some processes that have worked for various companies that I've had the pleasure to work with and help. Not all of the firms had the same processes in place. With this in mind, pick and choose those that are appropriate for you and your organization, modify them to meet your own needs, and determine how far you want to go:

1) Thoroughly analyze both your company and your competition. Consider core capabilities, strengths, failings, as well as market opportunities, etc. There are a number of effective tools and methods you can use for this activity.

2) Set up your Key Performance Indicators (KPI's), so you know what you're trying to accomplish. No more than five to ten max.

3) Have your budget in place at the beginning of the fiscal year.

4) Determine what your target market is, and stick with it.

5) Make sure you have at least one thing that differentiates you from your competitors. This should be consistent with the type of jobs you choose to bid.

6) Assess the capabilities and effectiveness of your field foremen and project managers. Assign a rating to each, indicating strengths/weaknesses, experience level by job type and size, and success at each (e.g., on-time completion, safety, etc.).

7) Analyze and rank every job you are about to bid to see if and how well it fits your market. Consider the general contractors you're most successful with, the competitors your bidding against, and the type of job it is. Have you done this type of job before, and did you make any money? Will implementing the *differentiators* make a difference in your bid?

8) Does this job fit with your Mission and Vision for the firm?

9) Is it possible to grow margin on this project? My goal was always to grow material and labor a minimum of 1% each. This was achieved by implementing preplanning and productivity processes and providing good training on both.

Let's stop at nine, just to keep this simple. Believe me, there are at least a dozen or more processes you can put in place, but too many will only make it too complicated.

After reading the preceding list, I'm sure you've probably started thinking about what you can incorporate into your bidding process to improve the quality of the bidding and to raise your closure rate to a much higher number.

Keep in mind, this has focused primarily on *bidding processes*. You will still need to have your *building processes* in place before you implement any of these goals.

I've seen business owners who, in desperate times, bid EVERYTHING that came down the pike, but they continued to lose the bids. They did hit some jobs, but often because they lowered their bid to beat their competitors, believing that if the other companies could bid jobs that low, they could, too.

When you're that tenuous in your business decision making capabilities, you do STUPID things and bid jobs on a wing and a prayer, HOPING they work out.

Most of the time they don't, and a year down the road there's usually one less PHVACR contractor around. I hope you're now starting to see the benefits of *Quality of the process + Quality of the product + Experience of the sale.*

As you progress through the book and read additional suggestions, I'm certain you will think of even more and better ideas that will contribute to your company's success.

If your ideas work, I only ask one thing in return. Please share them with the industry and give back a little to help make the PHVACR business a stronger and even more professional organization.

Before we move on to the next step, now would be a good time to ask yourself if you feel strongly enough about what you've read so far to really want to continue? As I said previously, implementing this six-step program requires commitment, dedication, and work. (Really trying!)

The last part - *work-* is usually where I lose a lot of people. They like the idea of changing how they run their organizations, but they never want to commit to doing the required work.

I remember reading a child's riddle once that asked the following question. *If five frogs are on a log and four decide to jump off, how many frogs are left?*

When I ask this question in seminars I conduct, I usually hold my hand up and show five fingers initially. By the end of the question, I fold down all but one finger.

Each time I do this, almost 100% of the audience responds with 'one' as the answer to the question. I believe that's because they are too quickly influenced by what they're seeing, before really thinking about the question. In fact, the answer is that *five* frogs are still on the log. The point made by the child's riddle is that *deciding* to do something and *actually doing* it are NOT the same thing.

The '*Six Steps to Success'* program and *A New Beginning* are all about change. They are a commitment to reinventing yourself and your organization.

It's about revitalizing the spirit within and creating excitement in your staff and *actually* 'jumping off' the log.

With the proper commitment and support of the leader, the team will embrace the opportunity to help reshape the company, will assume ownership of the change process, and will be a driving force in developing the processes and executing the change.

Do you like the size of your company, but you're disappointed with the bottom line? If so, this book can help. Perhaps you now want to grow your business. If so, this book can also help with that. Or maybe you just want to get your house in order so you can sell your firm and retire? This book can help you work towards that goal, too.

Maybe you just want to have more fun when you're at work every day. You want to see your employees (your assets) grow as individuals and to create more job opportunities within your company for them. Then this book is for you.

Now that you understand what *A New Beginning* is all about, and you have the basic data on hand, let's move on to step two –

"Building a Foundation"

6S = CS

$$6S = CS$$

Chapter Two

Step Two - Building a Foundation

Building a foundation. Now *that* should ring a bell to anyone in the contracting business.

By now you've gathered all the documents and papers that we talked about in step one - *A New Beginning* - and are ready to move to step two, *Building a Foundation.*

During the foundation step, you get down to the basics of your organization and determine if you really want to continue as you have in the past, to get out totally, or to reinvent your company and re-energize your team for what *can be* rather than what you currently tell them *needs to be*. This may sound deep, but let me assure you, I'm not that deep.

Simply put, you want to start by performing a SWOT analysis of your firm. Many of you already know about this tool. For those of you who don't, it means to thoroughly and honestly research and evaluate your organization's strengths, weaknesses, opportunities, and threats.

You can find a number of good articles on the internet and many books and other resources that will help you understand this process. Most of them provide the basics, and I urge you to take advantage of all the available resources. Just don't make this more complicated than it needs to be.

Since the results of this analysis will become input to the *Foundation* of your *New Beginning,* you must take this process seriously. Be thorough. This analysis will become a strategic tool in planning your future moves.

When I helped company teams with this process, we focused on what made their firm the best in the industry (e.g., people, brand, operations, marketing, technology, financial, etc.).

If your firm markets a product that no other company has, and this product differentiates you from the competition, then this could be one of your strengths. Get the idea?

As you and your team work through this process, keep the conversation open and just let the ideas flow. I promise you that you'll get through this just fine and will be pleased with the outcome.

Let's say you now have several items listed as major strengths that you feel separate you from your competitors. My guess is you've listed: your people, your brand or reputation, your professional office staff, skilled and knowledgeable technicians and field staff, the high-tech equipment in your shop that makes you more competitive, your pricing structure, or your marketing techniques.

If you have these types of items listed, you are on the right track. In fact, many firms consider these to be strengths.

Don't make your list too long. As I said, the simpler it is, the better to focus on the overall picture when you get done. If you identify more than six items, narrow it down to a maximum of six.

Next, list your weaknesses. Oh, come on. Yes, we all have weaknesses.

When you really get down to it, this list is usually the longest. I've found a couple of things you can do to get the most out of your staff when asking for their input.

One method is to have each person record his or her thoughts and have someone else read them aloud to the group. Then allow a few minutes to debate whether to add it to the list. Consider if it is really an organizational weakness or just a deficiency that can be corrected easily.

Brainstorming is another technique you can use to capture ideas from participants. Ask each person to share one weakness, and assign someone to record and display it for the entire group to see.

After going around the table twice to maximize input, the group debates the ideas for five minutes. Then everyone votes and selects which of the items are the true weaknesses.

The faster you go around the table, the better the ideas, because people don't have time to overthink them. They say the first thing that comes to mind, which is often the most significant idea.

You can use these techniques to help you capture the ideas for all of the SWOT categories. Again, try to keep the ideas on each list to a maximum of six or at least a manageable number.

If team members can't contribute an item when it's their turn, just move on. Hopefully, they'll have an idea when you come around to them the next time. If not, that's ok, too.

It's OK to pass over people who can't think of an idea quickly, because they are frequently the people who have great ideas when you return to them.

They just prefer to think through what they want to say before saying it aloud. Others will be very comfortable with sharing ideas the first time around.

Some of the weaknesses I heard identified during numerous company outings include:

1) Marketing materials are weak and not consistent across all business lines or products.

2) The brand is not that well known, or one division of the firm is currently being promoted over all the others.

3) Pricing, along with the overhead, is too high when compared to the competition.

4) Skilled and knowledgeable technicians and staff are in short supply; shop equipment is outdated; training programs are ineffective, etc. Get the idea?

In many of my meetings, some of the items were listed as both strengths and weakness, which is fine. Often, they do belong on both lists, so don't be afraid to go ahead and write them down.

Next, focus on opportunities. The list of opportunities is usually short because most of your staff are so focused on what they *should* be doing, they don't have or take the time to think about what they *could* be doing to improve operations and really differentiate your company from the rest.

Things you might expect to see on this list include: grow market share, penetrate more markets, differentiate yourself more effectively, provide more value-added services, cut overhead to be more competitive, get better tools, trucks and equipment to help improve productivity, improve safety, etc.

As you write these down, you'll immediately see a pattern developing that interlinks the SWOT lists. That's what you want to see - it's a good thing.

And the last, but definitely not the least, category to address is threats. What constitutes a threat? Well, the items that I see listed most frequently include: competitors, economy, lack of customer awareness of company services, market size (small town or too large of a market), etc.

You should now have comprehensive data to evaluate, and you can start to strategize and plan what you need to do to *capitalize* on your strengths, minimize or *eliminate* your weaknesses, *go after* your opportunities, and *address* your threats.

The outcome of this planning can now be used as your foundation for starting to rebuild your organization using strategic preplanned steps, over a measured period of time, with built-in stops that allow you to continuously evaluate the progress and outcome of each step.

This process will also highlight areas that may require you to take a new tack if/when necessary. Remember, never carve anything in stone unless you intend to live with the outcome for a long time.

Use the data to structure thoughtful and meaningful goals, and make sure your goals pass the SMART test.

SMART goals and objectives have been around a long time, but I have worked with very few people who actually used them. Once again, I encourage you to take advantage of the wealth of information that's available out there to better understand SMART goal criteria. This task falls into the *Really Trying* part of my 'six steps to success' formula.

Many people struggle with drafting goals and objectives that pass the SMART test. But once they do it, they realize that it isn't that difficult, and the effort is worth it.

Basically, a SMART goal should be (S) specific and clearly state what needs to be achieved. It must be (M) measurable, so that progress can be tracked and results known. It must be (A) achievable and attainable. Additionally, a goal should be (R) realistic and able to be achieved given the environment, your resources, and other considerations. Finally, the goal must be (T) time specific and detail when completion is expected.

Remember to also specify *when, who, what, how*, and *why* when putting together the detailed plans you'll need to meet each goal.

This test will help ensure that what you're trying to accomplish can, in fact, be achieved, and you'll know exactly what to expect, and by when. Because you can track progress, you're positioned to make adjustments, if needed, to ensure success.

Now that your SWOT is complete and you've set some SMART goals with supporting detailed action plans, you have the *Foundation* upon which to build your *New Beginning*.

At this point, if you stopped your retreat or work session and allowed a few weeks to pass before having the next one, you would have time to reflect upon the results of your first meeting and ensure that this *Foundation* will sustain you through your *New Beginning* process, and into the future.

I grew up working in my dad's auto repair garage. I remember lots of times, after I told him I thought I was *done* working on the customer's car, he'd come over and inspect my work. He would look under the hood, then start to yell at me. He'd say, "I've told you a thousand times to *step back* and look at your work to make sure it's correct before you assume you're *done*!"

Looking back, he was right about the *stepping back* part, but I'm not so sure about his yelling at me. After all, I was just a kid. But his point did stick with me throughout my life.

My point is, as you move through the six-step program, you need to stop along the way and make sure the processes you develop are being *done* or executed correctly. (*Step back!*)

You don't have a stick with a star on it, so you won't always be right.

By evaluating each step along the way, you can minimize the corrections you will need to make to your plans down the road.

I've always believed in the formula, Six Steps + Quality of the process + Quality of the product + Experience of the sale = Contracting Success, and by sticking to this philosophy, I've been able to see things from different perspectives.

Everything you do affects something else in your organization!

Every process and procedure you put in place will have an impact on the bottom line. If it doesn't - do you really need it?

This could be as simple as posting a sign on every construction trailer listing start times, break times, and quitting times, along with what start time really means. (e.g., We start at 7:00 AM. This means at your place of work with your tools ready, not driving through the gate, etc.) Having only this sign could increase your productivity by at least one percent.

Once you've completed the SWOT analysis on your own firm, analyze your competitors, using the same technique. Limit this to the top two companies in your area that you admire.

Be sure to record all of their features and the benefits they offer, and then list yours as well. Focus on the areas where they are superior to you. For example, they always get the $100,000-$500,000 jobs they bid, and you are usually third.

This indicates they have dominance in a niche market that works for them.

Maybe your tactic could be either to stay away from projects within this size range or to find ways to become more competitive on them. For example, are you picking the right foreman and project manager team? Have they been successful on these project sizes/types? Maybe you're not spending enough time preplanning these jobs, or you think they're too small for prefabrication processes?

See where I'm headed? Just take the time to study the market closely, and you will soon understand what you need to *do* or *not do*.

While you're taking this break to think about the results of your planning meeting, you need to make sure your *Mission* and *Vision* statements are still appropriate for your new, revised strategic plans.

If they're not appropriate, you should be willing to draft new ones that align with the revised goals for your company. If you don't have *Mission* and *Vision* statements, draft them now and be ready to present them at your next strategic planning *New Beginning* meeting, so your staff can provide INPUT and give their APPROVAL.

Now that your strategic planning and goal setting results are aligned with your M*ission* and *Vision*, it's time to schedule your next retreat or work session.

Before you leave for the session, have your accountant or comptroller compile a spreadsheet that captures the financial history of your company.

The spreadsheet should provide the comprehensive financial details you want and need to see. You could also have another version available that offers information appropriate to share with your staff.

In most cases, however, everyone benefits from seeing the same information. Always include a minimum of five years of historical data.

Spread out the results over twelve months and show each division's or department's results, one on top of the other, with the first grouping being revenue each month as compared to budget.

The second grouping should show gross margins, overhead, and net profit by department. On the right side of each, show a total for that year and the combined revenue and gross margin of the company.

What you're trying to do here is display the data in a way that allows you to efficiently compare your company's actual performance to the current budget and, if possible, to your company's key performance indicators (KPI's). Every company needs to have a set of KPI's to measure and evaluate performance.

In addition to periodically benchmarking your firm against industry standards and/or other companies, you can use this formatted historical data for regular internal benchmarking activities.

Recall the previous section on the importance of structuring SMART goals and objectives. To be meaningful, goals must be *measurable.* My experience shows that when your department managers know something is being measured, they will usually meet or exceed that particular goal as opposed to one they know you're not measuring.

In the service sector, the measures might be revenue per employee and/or technician, gross margin per employee, revenue per man hour, net profit per man hour, hours worked safely, etc.

For the mechanical contracting side of the organization, the measures could be productivity or gross margin by project manager, graded on a curve of the amount of revenue he or she is managing. For example, once a particular manager reaches five million dollars in revenue for managed jobs, does his/her gross margin drop by 15% or more?

Use whatever works for your situation and whatever you feel comfortable measuring. By putting this information in a format that reveals patterns, you can *learn from your past to plan for your future.*

In this format, you'll also be able to see if your past goals (budgeted revenue, margins, etc.) met the 'A' or *achievable* requirements to be SMART goals. My guess is that your departments missed their goal more than 50% of the time? If they did, look again at the goals. Were they even *realistic* ('R' requirement in SMART goals)?

Experience shows that almost all companies heap too many unrealistic goals onto the departments, or they push the departments to agree to take on more work than what's realistic or achievable. Most managers, not wanting to disappoint their bosses, often just agree to the goals.

In the end, the department managers become depressed because they are not able to deliver on the goals they committed to meet.

They might feel defeated and *underappreciated* for the effort they *did* make. They could eventually leave the company because they believe they lack the ability to manage the department to the satisfaction of the owner.

I believe this is one of the main reasons good people leave organizations!

In fact, the owner might be secretly saying: "He delivered more than I would have expected. I'm so glad I pushed the revenue or margin numbers higher."

This type of boss has no clue about the level of harm he or she is inflicting on the employees, as well as the possible future leadership of the organization. If your goals don't meet the SMART test, then don't implement them! This is why you need to have the financial history available prior to the next retreat. It'll show you the budget goals you established in the past and how each department did in achieving them.

If some departments are meeting goals and growing revenue at 15% per year, then it makes sense to set similar goals. But even though some departments are only showing growth at 5%, that doesn't mean the departments aren't trying.

It just shows that there's opportunity to dig in and evaluate the product mix they are selling, the margins they are delivering, and the support the company is giving them to succeed. It may just be that the marketing budget is not there for expansion, or that the market is over saturated with the current products they are being asked to sell.

One topic of interest that most business owners talk to me about is the distribution of overhead to each of the departments. Each firm does it differently, but almost every company I've worked with didn't understand the whole picture when applying overhead to their departments.

Most go by the budgeted revenue of the department, divided by the *total* company revenue, to determine the percentage of overall overhead to apply to the individual department. The departments are also asked to carry their own overhead (e.g., salaries, warranty costs, advertising, etc.)

Let me see a show of hands if you do it this way? WOW, almost 100%!

Now let me tell you that most, if not all, of you could be doing it wrong. Just ask the department heads responsible for trying to generate the net profit you're asking them to deliver.

Most are delivering the gross margin, but can't meet the net profit. This should tell you that the overhead distribution is too high for their department!

Why is this? There are several reasons that need to be addressed in your upcoming meeting or retreat. They are usually a combination of the following:

1) Unrealistic revenue goals set for the department, thus causing a push by the manager to get higher margins to offset lower revenues and still try to make net profit. The

result is a loss of work because they bid the margin too high for the product or market they are selling in, and everyone fails.

2) Unrealistic margin goals based on the mix of products or services they are expected to sell. Every product (e.g., residential service, commercial service, changeouts, etc.) should have their own gross margin and percentage of the total revenue, calculated out and totaled for a *combined* gross margin target. Don't set unrealistic goals!

3) Unrealistic overhead based on being pushed to deliver higher revenue, margins and net profit to help the other departments lower their margins and get more work. This one is used frequently. As an example, the service department overhead should *never* be higher than 25% - 30%.

These create a lose-lose-lose for the company, your employees, and your clients.

Owners must be realistic when setting goals for departments. They should sit down with the managers and help them set goals that will stretch, but not break, them. Yes, you can set stretch goals, as long as history supports that it is possible.

By doing so, the owner will develop a feel for where the company overhead should be and manage the firm accordingly. Department managers will not be burdened with trying to meet unreasonable and unrealistic goals.

During good times, the overhead grows, and what typically happens when business slows down, is management is too slow to shrink the overhead to match the new revenue levels.

With proper measures or processes in place, a good owner will manage the overhead to a level that stretches the managers, but does not put them in a no-win situation. Yes, it's a balancing act, but it is not impossible as long as the proper quality processes are in place.

My rule of thumb is to always set the company overhead for the average of the three or four lowest months' revenue of the previous year, multiplied by twelve. You can play with what works best for you. This should not only apply to the company as a whole, but also the individual departments.

Using this calculation will allow you and your staff to be stretched, but you'll also be meeting goals and meeting the net profit needed to grow your business moving forward.

Also, your bonding company will like the fact that you're meeting your financial obligations. They'll appreciate that your books don't reflect lots of fluctuation from month to month. This will also support smoother cash flow!

Additionally, you'll be managing your business soundly and not growing your overhead too fast. This keeps your current employees challenged and, also primed for professional growth and advancement in your organization. Now *that's* effective leadership!

One very useful tool you can compile and use to make sure you're not over or under stretched is a model organization spreadsheet. You can develop one using information gathered from a variety of sources, such as peer groups to which you belong or organizations within the industry that have been recognized for excellence.

This will help you develop your budget and staffing plan for the coming year and will ensure that you're capable of meeting those goals. It might also show what the revenue is per technician or crew for your residential, commercial, contract, energy management, fire protection, or other key department, based on historical data, as compared to peer groups or industry standards.

On the next few pages, I've provided ratios that I learned early on in my career. They have served me well when managing my own departments and companies, as well as other firms I've helped along the way. These ratios are just guidelines and can certainly be tweaked to meet your particular needs. Overall, they worked very well for me.

Your model organization can also incorporate your maximum staffing required to meet these goals, (e.g., ratio of 3:1 for field vs office staff excluding the shop and sales staff). The 3:1 ratio (field to office) works for service departments. For mechanical contracting, I use 4-5 office staff for up to three million dollars in revenue, then one additional employee per one-million dollars in added revenue.

I've never lost money for a company or corporation when I set up the next year's budget to reflect these ratios, plus the average of the three lowest months' revenue from the previous year, multiplied by twelve. This becomes the *break-even* revenue for the following year. Here's an example of a simple calculation

Previous year's lowest three months of revenue = $150,000 + $130,000 + $120,000 = $400,000/3mo. = $133,333/mo. X 12 months = $1,600,000 +/- next year's break-even revenue.

Keep in mind, this is not your budgeted revenue, but rather the break-even or lowest estimated revenue you should expect next year. So, what should your overhead be to ensure you at least break-even?

First, you'll need to know what gross margin you expect to earn next year. The easy way to know that is to take a look at what you did in previous years.

Does it look like a valid historical number or did you just end a few great years or poor years?

Again, I would calculate the *average* gross margin percentage for the *last three years* (e.g., 44% + 46% + 45% = 45% average gross margin).

With this in mind, let's say you just ended your current year with an overhead of $800,000 and 45% gross margin. If you divide your overhead by your gross margin, you get $800,000/.45 = $1,777,777 break even revenue.

By comparing $1,777,777 to your projected break-even revenue number of $1,600,000 from the previous example, you see that your overhead is too high and needs to be lowered.

For this example, you can determine a more appropriate overhead number by multiplying your break-even revenue ($1,600,000) by your projected gross margin percentage (45%). This results in an overhead calculation of $720,000.

This means you need to lower your current overhead of $800,000 to a number closer to $720,000 +/- to ensure that, at the very minimum, you meet your break-even number the following year.

If you manage to do more revenue at the projected gross margin, you'll end the year in the black. And believe it or not, this is why you are in business!

This is the point at which most owners and managers must determine if they are truly leaders. Do they have what it takes to make the tough choices required to cut the overhead, which will support the survivability of the company?

Remember that overhead is not just limited to personnel. Every department or area of the business can reduce waste and costs and increase productivity, so look for these improvement opportunities first. Also, consider your organizational structure and hierarchy, and make necessary changes.

If you're familiar with the 5S methodology and/or the principles of lean construction, this is the place and time to implement them into your organization to help maximize efficiencies. If you're not familiar with them, please take the time to research and learn about them. Consider engaging a consultant who specializes in these areas to help you implement them within your organization. You'll be glad you did.

However, despite taking all of these actions, you could still need to reduce personnel to meet goals.

This is never easy. However, as a leader you must take all necessary actions, *using appropriate processes*, to make sure you have the right people in the right positions.

Be a leader; be proactive!

Taking all of these actions helps position you to either break even (worst case) in the next year or to *always* make money! What a great concept!

You wouldn't send your foreman or service technician out into the field without the proper tools, would you?

By now you should realize how important it is to develop the *Quality of the process* tools needed to ensure the *Quality of the product*. Remember to always do your homework and *really try*.

I've interviewed with a number of firms during my career, and what they didn't know was that I wasn't there just to be interviewed. I was also there to interview them and see how they managed their firms, to review their financials, and to see what type of culture they supported in their companies.

I always did my homework prior to the meeting by calling local companies they did business with and, of course, by doing a detailed search for information using the internet and other resources.

I wasn't looking for a *perfect* company, because they don't exist. I was looking for a firm that really needed my help and where most of my six steps had not been implemented.

This spelled *opportunity* to me, and that's the firm I usually went with. I know, it sounds crazy, but I always felt I would be better positioned to add value to these firms and could contribute to their success.

I remember interviewing for a top position in the PHVACR division of a national consolidator that was owned by a utility company. I flew to their headquarters to meet with the divisional president and found that the vice president of the utility company had also flown in to observe the interview.

As I've previously shared, I was always prepared for interviews because I did my homework in advance. I went into the interview knowing that this particular consolidator was in trouble because their business models were flawed.

This company, like almost all of the other consolidators at the time, knew how to purchase firms. However, they seemed to struggle with how to manage them, achieve their promised economics of scale, and leverage best practices.

During the interview, I listened politely and answered their questions until we got to the part when they asked me, "Do you have any questions?"

"I only have a few" I said. I've researched the industry and have noticed that most, if not all of the national consolidators know how to grow their business through acquisitions. But when it comes to bottom-line results, almost all of them are failing. What makes you different from the others, and what are you doing that separates you from them?"

Well, the president of the firm stared at me and appeared somewhat embarrassed because he didn't have a good answer for me. On top of all that, he was sitting there next to his boss. He stuttered and murmured out the classics like, "We deliver quality service, and our technicians are fully trained, etc."

I responded with: "Every national consolidator claims to deliver those same things. What I'm looking for is what are you doing to guarantee the bottom-line results that the others can't?"

Well, as you might imagine the conversation got very quiet, and he gave me a very long, rambling answer that sounded very presidential, but was as hollow as an old, dead tree.

A few days later, I called the company to see if they had any additional questions for me and to find out when they would be making a decision. I wasn't surprised when they told me that the president was no longer with the firm and that the position for which I interviewed had been withdrawn.

Within a few months, the national consolidator was split up and the smaller, individual PHVACR companies were either closed or sold back to the original owners.

To make matters worse, within another relatively short period of time, the utility filed Chapter 11 and was looking for a buyer.

The point is this. As an owner or officer in any business, you must constantly do your homework and know your business inside and out. Be prepared to answer the tough questions! (By *really trying*!)

Whenever I was hired to help a company, the following usually happened.

I would come on board and give it my all, and the company would show a substantial improvement in revenue, margin, profit, safety, and productivity.

Then, over time the owners would start to feel intimidated by the amount of work required to really make it. They were either unable or unwilling to sustain the level of effort required. At this point, they usually reverted to their *same old way* of doing business. Why? Because it was easier!

Or put another way – the old way was less work!

Yes, change is hard. If you're not ready for it or you're not committed to it, then don't do it.

Culture is the essence of an organization. It will either make the company successful or destroy it. To successfully implement a culture change in an organization, the leadership must play a key role, or the change will not succeed.

Over the years, I've gathered lots of information, from multiple sources, about how to manage change. Understanding the stages of the change process are very important to implementing successful change in any company.

Moving from the stages of *denial* to *acceptance* to *action* is a long process if you don't understand what happens to people along the way.

With help, I've implemented change in many firms and moved through the process almost seamlessly by understanding and recognizing what people go through and what they need to support them along the journey.

By understanding the symptoms, you can help move the process along more quickly and get to the *action* stage sooner. Some experts say that changing or shifting culture can take years. However, I've seen the shift happen in as few as seven months with the right leadership.

I know what you're thinking! This is more than you want to get into, and you think you'll stop reading and stick with what you've always done. Right?

Again, it always reverts back to taking the path of least resistance -- or *Not Really Trying.*

Please don't get too caught up in the intricate details of change management. But do invest some time and resources in learning the basics and how to navigate them. I strongly recommend that you consider hiring an expert to help you.

As a leader, you must understand change management, so commit to doing whatever it takes to support the organization.

Who knows. You may actually enjoy it, and learn something along the way.

Change is not something to be afraid of. It's something to embrace.

I once spoke at a national convention, and after my presentation, I had the opportunity to sit next to a gentleman from our industry (PHVACR). He talked about how he had sold his business a few years earlier and how he had stayed on to help during the transition. My experience is that most owners who sell their businesses tend to do this.

Later in our conversation, he started telling me about how the cultures of the two firms were so different, they were impossible to merge together. And that it ended up destroying his lifelong work.

What a terrible feeling that must have been.

I saw the same issues occur with almost every single firm purchased by the national consolidators when the consolidators tried to incorporate their cultures into those of the newly acquired firms.

They started by *telling* the owners, who agreed to stay on through the transition, what to do and how to run their businesses, without any regard for the existing business model or culture that had made each company successful in the first place.

Don't get me wrong. All businesses can improve, but not with the tactics that some *(not all)* consolidators were using or employing at the time.

They treated all the contractors as though their businesses were identical, when in fact, they were all in different markets and different businesses.

By different businesses I mean they each had different 'products' other than 'contracting' that they offered their customers. Each company had developed different types of relationships with their customers, and they also operated in a different market or region of the country.

I remember the situation in my career when a larger company came along and purchased the smaller one that I worked for at the time.

The first thing they did was invite the executives to their headquarters to interview for the positions they currently held. Oh boy, I love interviews! I did my homework and went prepared.

When the day arrived, I traveled to the company and began the interview process in their main conference room, which was located on the top floor of their large headquarters. I started with their lowest level executives and worked my way up to the new CEO by the end of the day.

Keep in mind that this new company was not from the contracting world. They were primarily a venture capital firm, and this business was a new market for them. Also, the new CEO was not from the contracting industry.

We asked each other questions for about an hour. When the interview ended, to allow me time to catch my flight home, the CEO walked me to the elevator and asked me one last question.

He looked me in the eye and said, "Bill, my last question for you is this. Do you think I can turn the company we just purchased around?" Well, I looked him straight in the eye and said, "Absolutely not!"

At this point, as you might expect, the blood vessels in his neck got really red, and his eyes were throwing darts (poison ones) straight at me. After a long pause (for dramatic effect) I said, "That is, *unless* you surround yourself with people from the PHVACR contracting industry."

I said this because he disclosed to me, during our talk, that he had selected two new vice presidents to oversee the field operations across the United States. When I asked him about their qualifications, he said they had worked with him for years and helped him turn around many companies they had acquired. But none of them had been PHVACR firms.

I told him I believed most people from venture capital firms could not easily run a contracting business. (Although I honestly believe some people from the contracting world could manage a venture capital company.) I said if he surrounded himself with people from the PHVACR contracting industry, he would greatly improve his chances of succeeding.

Needless to say, that didn't go over very well with him, and he also didn't listen to me. The elevator door closed, and we didn't have much conversation after that. As I said before – I may not know what to do to fix all businesses, but I do know what *not* to do.

Within a year, and after another three CEOs, the company finally settled down and was resold to another capital management company.

Stories aside, our business is complicated and has many facets to understand. We in the PHVACR contracting world know that our business is *relationship* driven. Yes, our customers want and demand *quality, low price/value*, and *service* – but what they really want is to do business with someone they can *trust.*

They want to work with someone who has built a solid reputation in all the above, but also with whom they have had a good relationship in the past.

If they haven't directly worked with the contractor yet, they want to know someone who *has* worked with and developed a good relationship with that contractor. My experience with the service sector in our industry is that customers want and demand *excellent service*. Give it to them, and the price will not become the driving factor for future business.

Customers will call us back, not because we repaired their furnace or chiller. Almost any reputable firm in our industry can fix a furnace or chiller. They call us back because of the *experience of the sale.*

By that I mean, they were satisfied throughout the entire process, from the initial call into the office, to the account executive's speedy and complete proposal, to the technician arriving on time, to the follow-up call to confirm that the job was completed to their satisfaction.

It's about the *total experience.* If a contractor has the right culture ingrained in their organization, they will be successful.

Whether you're offering mechanical contracting, service, or any other product, if you deliver the *experience of the sale* correctly, you will have built a relationship with that customer for life, which is why we are in the business. Understanding the sales process is critical. People will continue to buy from you if they had a great *experience.*

They won't just remember that the technician was nice, or the sales staff was knowledgeable. What they will remember is that the *experience* of the entire sales process was easy and seamless, and they never felt stressed that they had made the wrong decision or suffered buyer's remorse.

Keep in mind, we don't *sell* anything to our customers. We provide a *solution to their needs* and a pleasant *experience* in the process.

Remember:
Six Steps (which also includes):
Quality of the process +
Quality of the product +
Experience of the sale =
Contracting Success

You've now laid the *Foundation* for your *New Beginning* and are ready to move to the next step. As you read the next chapter, please keep your *Foundation* processes in front of you and try to remember the basics of how you developed them.

You will be following a similar path as you move through the next step -

"Growth"

$$6s = Cs$$

Chapter Three
Step Three - Growth

Now let me clarify right off the bat that if you're expecting to grow taller, that's not what this step is going to do for you.

At least not in the physical sense. Figuratively, you may stand a little taller when you're through with this step, and I hope you do.

You should now be in a position to clarify what your *competitive advantage* and *competitive scope* should be.

That is, what are you going to focus on going forward and how are you going to get there? In other words, what is your strategy?

If you continue to bid every job on the street or continue to sell planned maintenance agreements (PMAs) to every customer out there, then the competitive scope side of your strategic goal falls into *cost leadership (cheap!)* while your competitive advantage side becomes *broad market (shotgun approach).*

This means that the business strategy you've chosen for your company focuses on *low price* with *no differentiation*. Is this really what you want?

Your strategy needs to be focused on a *narrow* market with *higher margins* and *differentiation* between you and the competition, as discussed in the previous step (less competition).

Step three, the *Growth* step, will help you get there, and you'll grow your business in the process. By growth I mean setting your organization on a path to success that follows the *Foundation* you've defined in step two.

Let me give you an example of what I mean:

1) You've identified your SWOT and that of your competitors, and you've established SMART goals.

2) You've laid out your historical past and identified where you were most successful.

3) You've identified and rated your foremen and project managers and can determine if you have the right teams for the right jobs. You've developed a method of rating your

targeted projects to make sure they fit your market goals and to identify if you have the resources to complete them successfully.

4) You now know where your niche market is and how to capitalize on it.

5) You've cut down on the quantity of jobs you bid and are now focused on the quality of jobs, which also improves your productivity.

6) You now have a 'bid it' process in place and are ready to start a 'build it' process to complement it.

7) You also now have a strategy to take your company forward.

8) You've aligned your staff, overhead, budgets and revenue expectations to meet the appropriate ratios.

During the *Growth* phase, you must focus your efforts and those of your team, to determine *what* you will do to get your market share of new work and *how* you will succeed in building and/or delivering the service you identified as your differentiator.

Let's say on the service side of your business, you've identified that the real growth in your market is in a category called *In Operation - Packaged Rooftop Equipment.*

Furthermore, you've identified that to be profitable in the sales process, you need to focus on a minimum of twenty tons and above per unit, per facility.

I picked this example because I studied this in various markets where I worked.

I identified the required market after talking with suppliers of this type of equipment. I discovered they had studies that showed the expected shipment on various size units over a 25-year period.

The studies showed that this size equipment would be in high demand during the next 3-5-year period because most of them were installed during a previous construction boom.

Well, the logical next step was to capture the PMA's for facilities with a minimum of twenty tons of cooling and more. By doing so, the company would be in the driver's seat as the *preferred contractor* when it came time to replace this equipment.

My study showed that the return on investment (ROI) for a 2-5-ton PMA facility vs. a 20-40-ton facility was 139% more gross margin over the life of the contract for the larger equipment.

Now, which market or customers would you want your account executives to spend their time pursuing, assuming it cost you the same amount per account in sales time?

It was an easy task to identify potential clients by looking at the ASHRAE standards and seeing the tonnage per square foot for different types of facilities.

Once I identified the types of facilities I wanted to target, the next step was to figure out what the potential market size was in our region.

Then I had to determine how much of that market we currently held and how much more we could grow this same market, over time.

By analyzing our technicians' capabilities, I determined they had the knowledge and expertise to handle most rooftop units up to and including 150 tons. The technicians who were only proficient in 10-30-ton HVAC equipment were targeted for additional classroom training to make sure we could still deliver *excellence* and a great *experience of the sale* as we grew this market.

Now that I knew what type of equipment would become our niche market (differentiator), I needed to investigate the size of the market in our area.

By obtaining a copy of a database publication (look for other similar publications, too), I could look at the number of employees per company and usually gauge how many businesses met the criteria that would fall into a 20-ton-plus business.

In these publications, most firms are listed as having 1-9, 10-99, or 100 and greater employees. They also provide a total number of businesses in the market area.

For one of our markets, I determined there were 35,500 companies that met our criteria. By assuming only 75% of the companies had PMAs, and knowing our average revenue per commercial PMA (including repair work), I was able to determine the size of the potential market (35,500 x 75% x avg. $$ PMA).

In this particular market, the average PMA was $1,500 per year, which equated to a potential market of $39,937,500 dollars per year!

Then I calculated the replacement market revenue, which was what I was going after. This added another potential $26,625,000 per year, based on an average replacement cost of $10,000 (low side) and assuming 7.5% of the 35,500 possible customers.

By looking at the market share we currently had (less than 2%), I was able to target the portion of the market I wanted to go after, based on our capabilities and growth potential.

I chose to go after 5% of the market over a five-year period.

Now that I had our strategy in place and the niche market I wanted, I needed to find a way to further differentiate (cost focused) ourselves from our competitors.

Before we move on, please keep in mind that even though this example details the structure for a service market, this thought process and approach can be applied to *any* business using similar data applicable to your specific industry.

Getting back to the example, the last thing I needed to do was compete against everyone else with the same standard PMA contract used by the rest of the industry.

Again, by going back and reviewing the research we completed on our competitors, I discovered that they all offered one-year PMA contracts with automatic renewals and with clauses to automatically raise prices (usually tied to inflation).

Now that sent up a red flag!

If I were an owner comparing PMA contracts from competing companies, what would I need to see to convince me to select one contract over the other?

Exactly - a fixed price.

By rewriting our existing contracts, I guaranteed our customers a fixed price for five years, with no cost increase and no penalty to cancel at any time if, for any reason, they were dissatisfied with our service.

Now, if I were a controller or purchasing agent for that company, I would go for the fixed price.

We reserved the right to raise our time-and-material rates once per year, and all repair work was quoted as a fixed price.

We offered our PMA customers a ten percent discount on material and labor, which was included in the proposal pricing.

Taking it a step further, I asked myself if one differentiator was enough to fend off the wolves? I presumed that within a year or two, the competitors would catch on to our fixed-price-for-five-years contract and would start to offer the same type of contract, too. And they did!

It just made sense that if we were going to get in front of the competition, we needed to stretch our differentiators. When our customers compared the PMA contract proposals submitted to them, they needed to clearly see where the *best value* was.

With that goal in mind, we decided to add high efficiency filters that were MERV 7 (2" and smaller) and MERV 8 (over 2") as standards to the PMAs. This would help with the customers' indoor air quality (IAQ) and help reduce the number of times they had to clean their office spaces.

The cost to add these filters was minimal, but the resulting benefits were highly effective. They added additional protection against compressor failure due to high head pressure and helped extend equipment life and lower energy and cleaning bills.

Next, we discovered that most of the PMAs in town offered coil cleaning as an added time-and-material provision, if and when the company discovered the coils needed to be cleaned.

When we thought about it, we realized that all coils needed to be cleaned once per year, just to protect the equipment and compressors and to help improve the IAQ and lower energy use.

We researched the market and found a multi-step process for cleaning coils that fit the bill, so we incorporated this service into the yearly PMAs.

Now we offered three distinct differentiators in our PMA contracts that separated our company from our competitors.

But was that enough to last the duration of the five-year contract so the customer wouldn't change providers? No. We really needed more.

I decided to get the company into the business of energy management, due to rising energy costs. Having this new business capability allowed the company to add yet another differentiator that helped separate it from the competition.

Keep in mind, these are all business strategies, and you will need to determine what works best for your particular situation and market at the time. Stay alert and understand that conditions can change quickly and frequently. I've used these same ideas on several different companies, with success at each.

The move to either enter or not enter this or any market can be determined from your SWOT analysis. List all the services you and your competitors currently provide, and then add to that list all the other services you can think of that would benefit your customers. By adding additional services that add value, you will have separated your company from the competition and raised the bar.

I like to use the phrase, *'sell the ranch, not the chickens.'* This means to always promote the entire company when talking to potential clients, not just one department.

A well-rounded organization that can design a project, provide building information modeling (BIM) services, build and maintain the structure, and provide continuous measurement and verification of its energy use is a nice *ranch* to be part of, and it should be promoted by all employees as they interface with prospective and actual clients.

Additionally, part of the growth process is about getting your house in order – literally!

Basically, get your entire facility cleaned and organized. Make it a place you would be proud to have your clients visit and tour.

Let your facility project an image that seems to say: *Look at us. We are professional at what we do, and our employees are proud to be working here!*

I'm sure you'd be comfortable inviting your potential clients to your home, even if you didn't have much time to prepare, because your home is probably always fairly presentable. Can you say the same about your business?

You shouldn't panic when you learn that visitors are scheduled to visit and tour your company. Your entire facility - from office, shop, equipment and storage yard, to parking lot should always be ready to welcome clients, *as well as your employees*.

The attitudes and morale of your employees will be positively influenced when they come to work each day, proud to be part of a company that cares not only about them, but also about the work environment and support they provide to their employees. This includes a nice facility, nice trucks, nice tools, the latest equipment and technology, and many other factors.

The word 'growth' congers up a number of meanings. If, early in the year, you tell your boss you're going to focus on 'growth', the first (and often only) thing he/she hears is that you're going to make the company a lot of money that year!

I know, because it happened to me.

I started working with a new firm and laid out the six-step program. I also put together a six-year business/marketing plan, which they approved.

The first year went as planned, as they laid the foundation for their growth. During the second year, I knew they needed to add PMA contracts to provide growth for the future, and they spent the year branding the service department as the value-added supplier for PMAs in their market.

This was done by developing a marketing and advertising plan designed to blanket the market and, also, by completely rewriting their PMA agreements. The goal was to grow their PMA market share by 100% in one year. This may seem like a stretch, and it was. But based upon my *Foundation* research, the market was large enough to make this happen, and we had the right tools in place.

All they needed to do was execute the plan, which is always one of the most difficult steps.

Well, the year went by, and they did grow the base PMA contract amount by over 100%. I was feeling pretty good because I knew the following year would be a record-setting year for the department and would contribute to the overall success and growth of the organization.

The problem was, the department didn't make much money during the first year of the *Growth* phase. They did make some money, but not the projected, dreaded budget amount.

The reason for the deficit was that their overhead was over 45%, but the department was projected to do only three million dollars in revenue. (Remember the previous discussion about overhead calculations and revenue of the department compared to revenue of the company?)

Well, the department made over 48% gross margin, which is in the 'best of the best' category for the HVAC service sector. But the overhead reflected a company that let its growth push its own overhead higher over the years. Without checks and balances in place, this imbalance was almost guaranteed to develop.

Now keep this in mind. To achieve growth of over 100%, the company had to spend a lot of money on advertising to get the branding they needed for their new *Foundation.*

When it came time to renew my contract at the end of the year, all I heard was, *"Your plan didn't make any money!"*

The owners seemed to overlook the reality that I had just helped them experience one of the best growth spurts that any company could ask for and had prepared the company's service department to have one of its best-ever years during the following year. I had also just established the firm as a leader in the service business in their market. They were now more than just a mechanical contracting firm.

As it turned out, I was vindicated the following year. The company had record revenues, margins, and the magical net profit, which was *off the charts*. Additionally, we managed to grow the service department PMA contracts another 100% from the base where they started, and yes, the company finally adjusted their overhead per the new business plan.

My point in sharing this story is to illustrate that, along the way in my six-step program, you won't always meet your goals.

But if you have open communication and if everyone on the team knows what the goals are and what sacrifices need to be made along the way, you will ultimately succeed.

The bottom line in the *Growth* step of the six-step program is this. Having and following a proper strategic plan, complete with goals and objectives, will allow you to grow your team and your company over time.

By improving business processes and by setting and following clear, achievable goals and objectives, your business will grow, and your culture will become stronger.

Your communication will become clearer, and your strategic products and services will be aligned to help build long-term relationships with your clients and your employees.

In addition to getting your house in order, you'll need to take the time to reevaluate your compensation scale for both your office staff and your sales staff.

As part of my program, I've often been asked to evaluate, recommend, and implement sales incentive plans. These plans can be all over the map.

For years, I've used what I refer to as the industry standard for sales, which is base salary plus commission, but I developed and added my own twists.

Yes, there are industry standards for sales. Although these generic standards are not developed specifically for the PHVACR industry, they work just the same.

As a former director of sales and marketing, I had to develop a fair but equitable plan, using base salary plus commission, that I felt comfortable presenting to the sales staff.

When considering compensation (excluding benefits) for your sales staff, the first item to define is percentage of base pay vs commission. This can be a little tricky, because different firms offer different ratios, and the ratios vary by market and region of the country.

As a starting point, I always used the 40/60 rule.

This means that 40% of yearly earnings should be base pay, with the remainder earned in commission. So, if you set the goal at $1,000,000 in sales and adopt the 10:1 ratio, sales staff should have the opportunity to earn $100,000 in income.

The base pay would be $40,000, 40% of $100,000. The commission would cover the remainder.

In my experience, structuring an effective commission plan for the remaining 60% presents the real challenge – and opportunity. I have always believed that in order to maintain a great sales staff, you need to offer an above-standard commission plan.

The plan should not only offer a decent living, but should also offer some type of opportunity for bonuses and residuals going forward.

Keep in mind, all markets and situations are different. That being said, the plan I used for this particular market is as follows:

1) Industry standard of 10:1 ratio. This means that if the salesperson sold $1,000,000 in revenue, they should earn a minimum of $100,000 or 10:1 ratio.

2) In addition to this, I also required a 4.5:1 ROI. If the salesperson earns $100,000, I would expect *no less than* $450,000 in gross margin (GM) or 4.5:1 ROI. (Goal was 45%.)

3) I incorporated a four-step bonus program in my sales commission plan. If the sales goal was $1,000,000 for the year, I assigned a certain dollar and percentage commission amount to the different products we sold, then allowed the sales staff to hit 50% of the yearly goals at the preset commission rate of 6%. All product sales and margins had to be met. This allowed the salesperson to earn 50% of his/her expected commission amount ($30,000).

4) In the second step of the plan, the commission rate would increase on the remaining $500,000 sales goal. In this example, the rate increased to 13%. This allowed them to earn a higher total salary. Again, all product sales and percentage GM goals had to be met. In this manor, they were rewarded for getting to their 50% sales goal sooner than later.

5) Then they moved to step three of the plan. In step three, the commission percentage increased, again for the next 15% of sales above yearly goals.

6) Once they met the goal in step three, the commission percentage went to its highest level on all sales over this amount, with *no sales cap*! This was step four of the plans.

7) With this four-step program, the sales staff was given the opportunity to earn above industry standard to approximately 12.5% – 13% +/- ratio to revenue, or approximately $125,000 - $130,000.

8) In the final piece of my sales commission plan, I offered my sales staff the opportunity to earn a 1% residual on all planned maintenance agreements, paid on the anniversary of each contract. With this

> final incentive, they could increase their base pay by remaining longer with the company and selling more PMAs. This would become a reason to stay with the firm and retain that income.

Because of this multi-layered plan, competitors offering only industry standard commissions had difficulty recruiting sales staff away from the company. Having a more comprehensive plan encouraged staff retention and, therefore, minimized the risk of departing staff taking customers with them.

I know there are many different ways of structuring and applying these plans, so you'll need to consider what works best for your market and region, as well as your competitors' pay scales. Hopefully, I've given you some options to consider and investigate further.

In addition to offering a solid commission plan, you must remember that your sales staff will need training on the new way of selling.

All sales staff are usually comfortable being trained on the products and services they represent and then going out and marketing and trying to sell them to potential customers.

That's the old way of selling. I believe in relationship selling, which is an entirely different way of approaching your potential customers.

The concept of relationship selling is represented in the equation as *Experience of the sale.* The goal is to ensure that the customer feels confident and comfortable dealing with your staff from initial contact to completion and beyond.

Your sales staff is key to building this relationship. First and foremost, they need to understand they are not selling anything! They are offering *solutions* to your customers' needs.

Using this approach helps the customer feel less pressured and more engaged when having an open conversation about their problems, and they are more receptive to hearing about potential solutions to their needs.

This reduces the stress level of your customer during the buying process and helps eliminate any buyer's remorse they might experience after the sale.

Remember, when providing business cards for staff, try to avoid the term 'salesperson' or something similar in the position title.

Unfortunately, many people have preconceived ideas about the term, so using an alternate word that better describes the broadened function that you're promoting could enhance the person's chances of connecting with the customer.

I called my team members account executives, which more accurately identified them as broader service providers.

They would meet with customers not only to discuss current needs, but also to set them at ease about the 'after-the-sales' process and the value of allowing the firm to help solve those needs.

During this time, they can talk about the capabilities of the entire company and the additional services or support other areas of the company can provide. Previously, I referred to this approach with customers using the following sentiment:

Sell the ranch, not the chickens.

Loosely translated: *Sell or market the entire company, not just your individual departments!*

Once customers feel confident that they have made the right decision in hiring your firm, they are less likely to shop around for another bid.

If they do get other bids, they'll realize the value of remaining with you, even if your price is higher.

Value for the Dollar and the *Experience of the sale* also equals *Contracting Success.*

In the beginning of this conversation about sales, I mentioned the products and services your firm offers to meet your customers' needs. I've been involved with service departments that offered their customers a choice of more than forty products. In my experience, this is way too many.

The number should rarely be more than ten so the customer is not overwhelmed with too many options and unable to make an intelligent buying decision.

I consider items like the following to be products:

1) Energy Benchmarks

2) Energy Assessments

3) Energy Audits

4) Energy Measurement & Verification

5) Energy Star & LEED Certification

6) Energy Management & Consulting

7) Several different types of Planned Maintenance Agreements

8) Repair and replacement products

9) Special projects work (is a product)

10) Special individual products that are exclusive to their firm (e.g., temperature controls, geo thermal, solar, etc.)

By now, you and your team have probably completed several retreats and multiple business meetings to strategize and develop your future plans.

Your team is on board, and most importantly, they see the passion and drive of their leader to make their company the 'best of the best' in the industry.

Please note that when I refer to the 'best of the best' in the industry, I really mean '*better than the best.'*

I never thought the 'best of the best' KPIs were good enough for our industry and always set my goals higher. By doing so, and by having the *Contracting Success* formula in place, I almost always managed to meet and/or exceed them.

Instill in your team that this new approach and direction is not just a passing fad that you read about in some book.

You've probably always had these thoughts in your head and really wanted to move forward, but this book helped open your eyes to the possibility of *what can be.*

Let's now move on to our next step –

"Stability"

6S = CS

Chapter Four

Step Four - Stability

Hopefully, you're still reading this book and aren't using it as a door stop. If you are still reading, I believe you're showing a commitment to improving your organization, and I commend you on your choice to see where this book might lead you.

Hopefully, I've enlightened you enough to want to participate in raising the level of professionalism within our industry (or any other).

If so, then let's move on to step four.

Stability can mean lots of different things. However, when you think of the *Stability* phase of the six-step program, think steadiness and firmness. Simply put, this is the time to bring all your efforts into focus for, and with, your team and to make sure everyone understands, and is on board with, the new direction and next steps. It is now time to implement and *stabilize* the changing strategies and processes.

With all the processes we have reviewed so far, we now need to make sure we implement them with steadiness and a conviction that they'll succeed.

You'll need to meet with your area managers or team leaders on a regular basis to give and receive feedback on how the implementation of the six-step program is progressing. Listen to them carefully, and be prepared to constantly take a new tack.

For those not familiar with the term tack, it simply means to change the course of a ship to catch a wind. You need to keep the wind in your sails to move forward and reach your destination. (Frankly, I've never been sailing, but I always wanted to use the term tack. It's kind of cool!)

Also, by meeting and listening to your staff, you'll begin to get a real feel for where the six steps are taking you. You've faced the challenges of analyzing your company and developing plans for improvement, and you're now executing the plans. Collecting and addressing all feedback is critical.

You'll discover, as I did, that training is a big part of the process. Your human resources personnel, or other administrative staff, should be enlisted to arrange training classes for all your employees, to ensure they are constantly updated on progress.

If qualified, they can also continue to train employees and reinforce the goals and processes that were developed during the previous retreats and other working sessions. This will help everyone stay focused and on course.

I've always made it a point to speak directly to the field personnel on the processes and explained the features and benefits of the program and what it means to them in the present, as well as in the future. In addition, I've taken the time to educate the field personnel on how their daily actions impact productivity and how they control most of the dollars flowing through the company.

I usually started by showing them how their productivity and feedback impacts the bottom line more than additional revenue, which in return creates job security. (See "Improve Your Productivity, Why?" chapter later in this book.)

Keep in mind, even if you are a small company with just a few employees, all of my steps still apply. Just on a smaller scale. The feedback I heard most frequently when trying to change the culture in an organization was, *What's in it for me?*

I always like to hear that question when rolling out my six-step program because it was so easy to show people what their future would look like.

Make sure you explain that there will be bumps along the way and that it won't be easy. But, once these processes are implemented, the end result will be like winning the super bowl.

Be sure to explain how they will benefit directly through job security and longevity. They'll also feel proud of what they do and, in the company, they work for.

I actually looked forward to talking with the staff about the changes we were implementing into their business model because my excitement, often directly transferred to them.

As the leader, you need to attend the training meetings to show your support of the teams and to emphasize their importance. You should actively participate in the sessions by presenting or facilitating part of the training.

Also, seriously consider involving your staff, both field and office, in providing the training. They are great resources and can help develop the programs, be presenters, coaches, mentors, etc.

I always liked the name of the training sessions to send a positive and motivating message, such as: "Company Name – Success Training" or something similar. Then, as each participant completed a training module, they would receive a certificate of completion and/or another type of recognition, often at a special luncheon or event. The possibilities are endless, so be creative.

One thing the CEO, president, CFO, COO, department managers, field supervisors, and others in authority must continually do during the implementation process is praise the staff for the progress and contributions they are making to the success of the company. As previously stressed, they must also constantly give and receive feedback about the processes being implemented.

Don't forget to listen to all of your employees. They are in the trenches, and their feedback can and will be invaluable. Also, remember to resist the temptation to tell them what to do.

As leaders, your constant presence will provide stability to the six-step program and your team.

This process will not be a short one, and you could be tempted to rely totally on your staff during implementation. However, without your constant encouragement, they will think you don't care, and their interest and efforts will fall short of success.

Please keep in mind that this is a team effort. All departments must work together.

Although purchasing, estimating, service, shop, field, office, human resources, accounting, sales, and all other groups will be working hard to implement their individual processes, all departments will need to meet together periodically to compare progress and to share and resolve issues.

The leader of the organization can help facilitate these meetings. Other department leaders, who have the skills to provide balance and support to the team, should also be enlisted to help.

As the gears of change turn and you start to see the successes of your efforts, you should celebrate your victories, no matter how small.

At one company, I mounted very large bells on the walls in each department for employees to ring every time they met a goal or got a job or satisfied a customer. And if they sold a planned maintenance agreement or met any of our *Foundation* or KPI goals, they were encouraged to ring it twice.

Now that doesn't sound like much, but at least we were celebrating our victories as we achieved them, because we worked hard as a team to bring them in.

Lou Holtz, a great coach once said, "Don't tell me how rocky the sea is, just bring the darn ship in."

In other words, your team will want to complain about the changes and talk about how things were easier the 'old' way, and they'll want to fight the changes along the way. That's normal and to be expected all through the change process.

In fact, it's a good thing!

Encourage their conversation, but keep them focused on the goals and engaged in the new processes. Make sure they always know about the progress being made and the successes being realized.

Over time, most of your employees will accept and embrace the new direction of the company. However, initially you'll have some team members who are on the fence, some who are on board, and some who will never accept the changes.

Focus attention on the members who are already on board, as well as those who are on the fence. The stragglers who don't want to accept the company's new direction are probably the ones who should have been addressed a long time ago. Now's the time to evaluate your resources and build your future team.

I've gone into many firms to help them out, only to encounter these stragglers that management should have taken care of prior to my coming on board.

Do yourself a big favor and address your personnel issues. Make the necessary adjustments, and move on. Until you do, you'll find it even more difficult to turn the firm around and implement change. The sooner you do it, the sooner you'll start to see the results of everyone's hard work.

In fact, when you make these shifts in staff, you may hear numerous employees saying, "Thank you, you should have done that sooner."

The stability phase of the six-step program could take a year or longer to fully implement and to get your team comfortable working together, rather than as individual departments, divisions or (to use a popular term) *silos.*

In fact, I would suggest that you stop using the term *division,* if at all possible. This word alone can reinforce disconnect and possibly discourage teamwork.

As I stated before –

Sell the ranch, not the chickens!

As the year progresses, you'll discover you have a more cohesive work family. They now view the company as something they belong *to* and want to work *with,* not *for*.

You'll see additional organizational growth, and your foundation will be stronger than ever.

Your stability or steadiness will be firm. Because of the new tack, your sails will be full of wind, and you'll be moving in a positive direction.

And the PHVACR industry (or any other business) will have one more truly professional organization as part of its membership.

As we move through these steps, each section gets a little shorter. But please keep in mind that shorter chapter length doesn't mean diminished importance of content!

In fact, the concepts of *Quality* and *Teamwork* have been included in all of the previous steps or processes, and their integration throughout is critical to achieving your goals.

*But…*now it's time to really focus attention on each of the remaining steps. We're almost there. Let's move on to step five -

Quality!

6s = Cs

Chapter Five

Step Five - Quality

Quality. Now *that's* a word I haven't used much in this book! (Just kidding . . .) *By now, you're probably tired of hearing it.*

Well I'm sorry, but I'm really excited about sharing this part of my six-step program because without *Quality,* we just can't reach a successful end.

The word is used twice in my equation: *Quality of the process* + *Quality of the product* or Qp + Qp, so it must figure heavily in my program. Right?

Well, you're right. Implementing quality processes throughout every aspect of the business directly contributes to your delivering quality products that meet customers' requirements, and our customers keep us in business.

I hope that the examples and scenarios described in this section will help you expand your understanding of what's possible and increase your resolve to look for and take every opportunity you have to help your company excel. Although the examples used might be specific to one area of the business, the concepts can be applied to all others. So, keep your minds open and the ideas flowing. Now let's focus on *Quality*.

Here's a list of actions that describe a *Quality* path that you and your company could be on:

1) Receptionist has been trained to handle calls professionally and can direct them to the proper individuals or dispatchers with ease.

2) Individuals and dispatchers have been trained to take calls professionally and serve the customer.

3) You've developed a quality "bid it" process.

4) Your entire team, both field and office, have been trained to provide exceptional customer service.

5) You're delivering the *Experience of the sale* (Es) in everything you do.

6) As a leader in your organization, you are championing the value and use of the six-step program, and you're guiding your team through the change process.

7) You have in place a business strategy that aligns with your vision, mission and values.

8) You've introduced new differentiators that will distinguish your firm from the others.

9) Your overhead is lean, and your managers are stretched, but they continue to enjoy their work, feel valued, and have time to regularly evaluate their effectiveness and direction.

10) You're now producing quality processes and work throughout your organization by having the right people in the right place, tools and equipment that improve productivity, correct incentives and compensation policies, properly trained and skilled employees, etc.

As before, let's stop at ten items, just to keep it manageable.

Ask yourself if your organization has been transformed to this stage yet. Is it what you were expecting, and does it exceed what you thought was possible? Hopefully, you answered 'yes' to both questions. If so, you're ready to raise, yet again, the quality level of your company.

I have always been a little obsessed with the details of everything I do, and these steps tend to reflect that obsession. Had I been different, I may not have been as successful in helping companies improve their organizations.

I've worked with many commercial construction companies, and I've learned that having effective 'bid it' and 'build it' processes will help carry you through to your ultimate success.

Unfortunately, for many of the regular or *typical* PHVACR contractors I encountered, the 'bid it' process focused primarily on the estimator's efforts. If the company got the job, they started their three-step 'build it' process when they 1) brought in and assigned the job to the next available foreman and project manager, 2) handed them the plans and 3) said, "Go build it - and by the way, we are already two months behind schedule!" Sound familiar?

Well, this book is about moving your company from *ordinary to extraordinary*. So, let's look again at these two critical processes.

We've already spent some time talking about the 'bid it' process, which impacts the quality of your bid and your success at getting work. Under the 'bid it' process, you have already reviewed and selected the best jobs to bid. You are using the foreman and project manager (PM) who are most qualified for each job and who, if possible, have previously worked with the general contractor. At a minimum, they have successfully completed a project similar in size and complexity to the new one.

As a result of this process, you've formed the team, which includes the estimators, project manager, and foreman. They will work the bid together, become thoroughly familiar with the job, and take ownership of the job after it's awarded to your company.

The 'bid it' process also lays the groundwork for your 'build it' process.

The 'build it' process starts when you've received the contract and reassembled your team. You're already ahead of the game because your key players are familiar with the project and ready to go!

WOW! Have you ever been that far ahead of the curve in the history of your firm? That's quality!

As nice as this feeling is, it's not enough to ensure success. At this point in the process, your next action would normally be to send the foreman and project manager out to the field to start construction. *But don't do it!*

Let's examine the 'build it' process again. But this time, we'll enhance the process by incorporating additional steps. As you read through this list, try to add some of your own ideas.

'Build it' Processes:

1) Bring your foreman into the office and have him/her take off the entire project again. That's right. Don't let the foreman use the estimator's job takeoff! How many times, when things go wrong on a project, are the estimators blamed?

2) Ask the foreman to take off the job in the sequence that he/she would like the materials delivered to the construction site or to your prefab shop.

3) Get your building information modeling (BIM) team working with your foreman and project manager to understand the project and to determine what and how much work will be prefabricated in the shop and delivered to the site and what work will be field fabricated.

   Don't let the foreman independently determine what gets prefabricated. Remember this -- Everything that can be prefabricated needs to be prefabricated. Everything!

   Think outside the box when it comes to prefabricating the project. Consider bundling the corridor mains or risers (both duct &

piping) on racks and delivering them to the field as one assembly for installation. Also consider asking other trades to come to your prefab shop to install their portion of the mains into a prefabricated rack system, so all trades are detailed, coordinated, and set in place as one assembly.

This works great for high rise projects! Just think of how much material handling you can eliminate. Both efficient and effective. *Quality again!*

4) Allocate a space within your office dedicated for all the foremen to use so they can do their pre-planning and other related tasks with the least amount of distraction.

5) Give your foremen the time they need to fully preplan their projects and understand how they will build them from the beginning through to the commissioning stage.

   Do not let them take off the project or do the preplanning in the field! If you do, they will be instantly and *constantly* distracted and could be seriously tempted to revert back to doing things using their old methods. As we all know, habits die hard, so insist they stay in the office to complete these actions.

6) When your foreman says that he/she is ready to start the build, call a meeting of your entire team and spend as much time as necessary having the foreman and project manager explain, in detail how they plan to build the job from beginning to end.

   Have another foreman and project manager who have either worked with this general contractor or built similar projects also attend the meeting to ask questions. Consider inviting the superintendent from the general contractor, as well as your subcontractors' foremen, to ask questions and provide input.

   At the end of this meeting, if the foreman still doesn't feel ready to go to the field, then allow them the additional time needed to prepare.

   Meanwhile, have the foreman select an assistant (or second) who will handle typical, early construction items in the field while taking direction from the foreman, who remains in the office.

7) Schedule and hold another meeting only after the foreman tells you that he/she is ready to 'build it.' (Not when you tell the foreman you've scheduled the next meeting.)

8) Hold the next meeting with the same team and ask the same questions. When you're finished, make sure the foreman says, "I'm ready to deliver a quality project!" Then, and only then, can he/she leave the office and start to work in the field.

At this point, your project manager and foreman are a team with a direction and a plan, and they are coordinated with purchasing, safety, detailing, the prefab shop, and all personnel involved in the project.

What a great feeling it is to know that your team has preplanned and prebuilt the project and has taken ownership prior to the project even starting.

What do you think the success rate of this project will be now?

****

I remember when I joined a mechanical contracting firm that belonged to a national consolidator. I was hired because the firm was in need of new leadership.

Even though the executives were intrigued by the 'Six Steps to Success' program I presented, they were very reluctant to let me change how the business was being run. As a result, we continued to bid every job out there and maintained an 8% +/- closure rate.

However, I didn't give up. I kept pushing the executives to try at least one project using the team approach while implementing my six-step program and business strategy.

Finally, a very large remodel project came to market. The job was larger than any remodel project this company had ever done, and they finally gave me the go-ahead to proceed.

I instantly assembled the team, picking the foreman, the project manager, and the detailing team prior to starting the bid takeoff.

We all agreed that the bid would be assembled no later than 3:00 PM the day before it was due, using plug numbers where needed. We would meet in the war room to review it in detail.

The war room was a designated space large enough to handle our bid team of around ten or more people. It was equipped to display bid information for everyone to see, and all the plans and specifications were readily available. We had dinner brought in, since we expected to be late that night thoroughly discussing and reviewing every aspect of the bid.

This included educating the foreman and others on 'units per day' from the estimator's takeoff, as they had never been exposed to what productivity included or what was expected of them daily.

As everyone began to understand the units included in the bid from our bidding software, they started to provide input to the amount of labor needed or not needed to install material. As it turned out, the bid team really did understand and know labor units. They just had never been asked to share their ideas with anyone.

At the end of our work session, we had 'built the project' from the ground up, including everything from staging the material to commissioning the project.

Prior to this work session all of us had visited and gotten familiar with the site, so when the evening was over, the team knew this project inside and out. We felt we had done everything we could to ensure we had a solid and accurate bid - nothing more and nothing less than it took to build the project.

All that remained was to apply the final gross margin we wanted to make and remove the plug numbers. Since I had already put together the overhead and margins required for each product in our firm, I knew we could bid this project at a tight number and still deliver the margins we needed. This would allow the company to meet budgeted cash flow goals for both the coming year and the next, since this was a two-year project.

I knew the competitors and the general contractors and had analyzed their strengths and weaknesses. I also knew how and where we could capitalize on this knowledge.

Well, the bid day arrived. We bid the project and waited for our project manager to notify the office with the results. You all know this is the toughest part of the job, but also the most fun. He finally called and said there were two bidders, and we were the lower of the two bidders. The bids were - (Wait for it!)

Half a million dollars apart. Wow!

I instantly knew we had a winner and was not overly concerned with the half-million dollars left on the table. We had done our homework, and we knew this project inside and out. We had gone through every line of the bid and checked everything two and three times. But you can guess the reaction from our corporate headquarters:

WHAT? Half a MILLION DOLLARS LOW?

Their initial, knee-jerk reaction was to say, "Pull the bid, and claim we made an error." I explained to them that our bid was sound, and I would stand behind it with my reputation. If this job didn't make money, I would turn in my resignation!

They waited a day and called me back. Understanding the impact this project could have on this company, as well as the corporation, they asked me one last time if I was absolutely confident that the bid was accurate, complete, and free of major errors? I assured them that I was!

They authorized me to proceed with the project and to continue my six-step program with the understanding they would be watching me closely.

Now, how many of you would believe in something so much that you would put both your own and the company's reputation, as well as your future, on the line?

As it turned out, the project was one of the best this firm had ever undertaken. The project came in ahead of schedule, under budget, and it made *lots* of money. Also, we finished with no safety violations.

But the best part was the employees becoming energized by the process. They had never been involved in a job to this extent.

They were asked to provide input to the bidding process and given the time to preplan the project during the 'build it' phase.

It was a new company with a *New Beginning* from that day forward, and incorporating this approach became the norm on how we did things.

In this case, I had done the homework and was ready to implement or execute the change, but no one would give me the chance because it was very different from how they had *always done it.*

The culture shifted, and change happened almost overnight.

We still had significant work to do, and I wanted input to the processes from the team to be incorporated into the steps. But it was easier than expected due to the quality of the team. This was, hands down, one of the best teams I've had the privilege of working with during my career.

I hope this book will help all people who are willing to listen and put in the work (*really trying*) enjoy the successes they deserve, and that it will provide a solid foundation to pass on to their employees and the next generation.

Hopefully, you've successfully implemented the first five steps of my six-step program (or even your own five steps that are better than mine!) into your organization, and you're seeing a new 'normal' way of doing business, using these steps

With an open mind and the willingness to always take a new tack when necessary, your firm will be around for many generations to come.

It's now time to move on to the sixth and final step of my six-step program -

"Teamwork"

$$6S = CS$$

Chapter Six

Step Six - Teamwork

Teamwork, as you have read in the previous chapters of this book, has always been an integral part of every process of my six-step program.

By now your teams have been working together and developing new methods and approaches (maybe even new 'steps') that will help make the company they work *with* the 'best of the best' in the industry. Time will pass, and even though the people and processes continue to perform, you might reach a stage where you feel that the organization is just *going through the motions*. No additional progress is being made and you haven't celebrated recently.

CEOs, COOs, CFOs and other organizational leaders tend to back away when they start to see benefits from the six-step program. They feel confident that they can reduce their involvement and focus their attention in other directions.

Early on, I stated you need to enjoy working, while still allowing time for yourself and your family. Remember you're not married to the company! Do you see a 'ring' around your desk?

Finding the right balance is always challenging. It's truly a juggling act that we all struggle to master, and I hope you have been able to find that balance in your life, but... *Yes, there's always a BUT!*

It's very easy to go a little too far at times and forget how you got to this point in your life.

You've worked hard to champion change in your company, you're reaping the results, and life is great. But you're seeing signs that maybe you've disconnected from the organization a bit too much.

Perhaps you've noticed that communication efforts have slacked off and old habits are creeping back in. You're sensing reduced levels of commitment from your teams.

You want stability, not stagnation! When this happens - and it probably will - it's time to reassess the situation, take action, and reenergize your teams.

Get them back together. Schedule additional retreats or work sessions dedicated to reviewing the organization's goals and performance, as well as the performance and results of all processes. Have your employees bring information about the processes they have implemented and new ideas on how to make them even better, so the organization is constantly improving.

Also, remember that the business environment, your market and competitors have probably changed. Analyze your company again. Gather more input, assess where you are and make adjustments. Make sure everyone understands where they're going.

Your employees have worked hard and need to hear from the leader that you appreciate their efforts. This is the time to reinforce your team's confidence in the new processes and to share the successes they've worked so hard to accomplish. With your renewed interest in their thoughts and on what works and what needs to be changed at this point in the six-step program, everyone will come together once again, and realize this truly is a *TEAM* effort.

As a leader in the organization, you now have the opportunity to show how one department's processes may have impacted other departments, and vice versa. As an example, maybe a customer was so impressed by a new process implemented in the service department, that the customer now wants the contract side of the company to design and build their new headquarters.

Or perhaps, because the contract side of the company did such an amazing job of constructing a new building on time and under budget, the owner now wants the company's service department to maintain it for them. See where I'm going?

When all the ‘chickens’ on the ‘ranch’ work as a team and generate business for the other ‘chickens’ as well as themselves, the entire ‘ranch’ succeeds. As stated earlier, every action affects the bottom line of the company. And this result can be linked to the *Teamwork* step in the six-step program.

Your team will feel appreciated and energized and willing to help provide new ideas for the betterment of the firm as a whole.

Although they may have drifted somewhat after feeling the initial successes of the program (just as management may have procrastinated in addressing overhead issues during good times), they have now come together with renewed commitment.

It’s important to have checks and balances in place that highlight the need to reassess your progress, and it’s equally important to reenergize teams. Without these triggers, these meetings will not take place, and your teams will drift apart. Also, the organization will not sustain all the good results of the team’s hard work. Now is also the time to reevaluate the members of the team who have been in charge of implementing the processes.

Just as you did with your foremen and project managers, you should be constantly rating your team leaders. You need to make sure they are still in the

20% of employees who really want to continue to move these changes forward.

Are they still engaged, or have they grown so weary of the processes that they are torpedoing them behind your back?

Yes, this does happen, and that's why, as the leader, you need to stay involved and constantly listen to your team leaders.

If your team leaders are disengaged, then meet with them one-on-one and find out why. The reason may be as simple as they need more direction, or as complicated as they feel they are not being respected for their efforts.

One of the most difficult responsibilities of a manager, regardless of level, is supervising people. As human beings, we don't like confrontation, but we still have to deal with it. Some managers are more skilled than others at addressing employee issues and at coaching and providing feedback.

I've found that some managers begin to back off the change process when they start to feel too much push-back from the team they manage. It's often because managers don't have the skills to communicate change properly to their teams, or to encourage their involvement.

Again, now is the time for you, as the leader, to find and resolve these issues. Perhaps additional training will correct the problem, or maybe you'll need to make a change in the team management.

There's an old saying: "If a turtle is on a fence post – it's because someone put it there!"

This simply means if you have managers in positions that they're not qualified to perform, it's often because *you* put them in those positions.

As an example, one employee – let's call him Bob - probably performed well as a project manager and successfully completed every job he ever touched on time and under budget, so you decided to promote him into a different management position, probably one having broader responsibilities.

He got all excited about the praise you were giving him and the higher salary you were offering and accepted the new position! Here's the problem. He may not have had the required skills and/or the proper training to handle the new position.

As I stated earlier, overseeing people is one of the most difficult responsibilities of a manager or team leader. Some people enjoy it and do it well, and some people just don't like it.

If you have employees who just don't like the responsibility of managing others and who aren't effective at it, then get them off the fence post as soon as possible, and find others within or outside your organization who have the desire and the skills needed to more effectively supervise others, as well as lead teams.

Often a new manager is put into a situation where he/she must deal with a person on the team who should have already been released or repositioned in the organization.

If you're aware of this situation, please don't shirk your responsibility by relying on the new manager to handle it. Do what you're there to do and lead. Make the necessary changes as quickly as possible to keep the *wind in your sails* (and in the sails of the new manager, too).

Teamwork, Teamwork, Teamwork! This is the engine of your firm. It drives the culture, the vision, the mission, and the values of your company, and without it you won't succeed.

Empower your teams, and they will inspire each other and impress you beyond your wildest dreams. Your people are your most valuable asset, and you need to treat them as such.

If you're a person who likes to be in control, ***please*** resist the urge to micromanage your employees. Point them in a direction; make sure they understand the goals, objectives and expectations; and provide them with guidance, feedback, support and the resources they need to succeed. Share your vision with your employees, and over time, it will become theirs.

In return, they will amaze you with their spirit and their drive to feel appreciated and part of such a great TEAM.

If you've implemented everything in this book, you should now fully understand the goal of the 'Six Steps to Success' and my simple formula of:

6*S* = C*S*

Six Steps =

"Contracting Success"

6S = CS

$$6S = CS$$

Chapter Seven
What is Success?

Hopefully, you and your team have embraced the 'Six Steps to Success' formula and are now working on integrating the processes into the business. Perhaps you're even adding to or modifying the steps and approaches to make them better *fit* your organization and more aligned with your mission, vision, culture and market.

Additionally, as a leader in your organization, you are learning that things don't need to always stay the same, and you have grown in the process.

A magic bullet or single formula that guarantees success simply doesn't exist. But if you keep trying something new and it works, then you're well on your way to improving and growing your company, and it may become the new *norm*.

I've attempted to write about and share the processes that have brought me success in my career, because I want to give back to an industry that has given so much to me.

I've always believed that success is what you believe it to be, not what someone else thinks.

For me, success was having the opportunity to work with so many great people in the engineering and PHVACR industry during my life and having many incredible experiences that helped me learn *what not to do,* and fortunately, to learn *what to do.*

Additionally, I've always believed that one should work hard, enjoy life, and give back. This book is my 'give back.' I've had a long career in this industry, and have often looked for resources about the business. Over time, I've discovered that there are many great business books, but very few books about this *specific* business and the experiences we all have had.

If you're like me, you have had your ups and downs, and you keep getting up again. After all, as I said previously, I believe that contractors are born optimists. It's hard to keep us down!

For me, success is also about being resilient – that is, about getting up again and again, but learning something each time. It's about trying my best at whatever life throws my way, while still maintaining a balance between my home life and my career.

So, what is success to you?

It's whatever you want it to be. Do you stop here? Do you continue down the same road? Do you share your experiences with the rest of the industry?

Do you now pass your knowledge on to the next generation? Do you continue to grow?

I'll leave you to define 'success' your own way. But in my experience, if you and your team have made it this far, you can pat yourselves on the back.

Thank you for allowing me into your firm….

Don't stop reading.

More great lessons are yet to come!

6s = Cs

Chapter Eight
My Dog, Rambo

"Let me walk into the wall, Daddy."

Rambo was the name of one of my two golden retrievers. The other was named Cooper.

This particular story is about Rambo and how his personality changed when our Cooper passed away from a heart condition.

Rambo was a very loyal and smart dog and a beautiful golden retriever. His breeding record showed that some of his ancestors had earned championships in either conformation or field trail, so we knew he was probably a well-rounded dog. And he was.

Rambo was the more subservient of the two dogs and would often defer to Cooper when he was around. He almost always let Cooper have the toy he wanted or get his 'treat' first.

Don't get me wrong, Rambo could hold his own against Cooper, and for the most part, they were buddies for life.

Cooper was nine years old when he passed away suddenly while on our Saturday morning walk to the local park where we would play ball, then sit in the Gazebo to rest and enjoy the ducks on the pond. That was a sad day for my wife and me because Cooper was part of our family.

Throughout his life, Rambo always wanted my attention and to be next to me. He had to try harder than Cooper for that position because Cooper would always nudge him out of the way. But throughout the nine years we had Cooper, Rambo never stopped trying to get that coveted position next to his 'daddy.'

Rambo would always fetch the stick first, bring it back to me, then sit in front of me waiting for me to take it and praise him for his effort.

Many times, even though Rambo got to the stick first, Cooper would manage to steal it away from Rambo and bring it back to me, expecting the same praise. Sometimes they would bring the stick back to me *together,* with both of them hanging on to it for dear life. Each one wanted to be the dog I praised first.

After Cooper died that Saturday morning, Rambo's personality quickly changed, and he became a totally different dog almost overnight.

He instinctively knew that he was now next in line after the alpha (me), and he immediately became my shadow.

He did everything he could to gain my attention and remained at my side constantly as if to say, "I'm here for you, Daddy, now that Cooper is gone, and I won't let you down."

Well, time passed, and Rambo got older and developed cancer. During his last two years, he was totally blind, and my wife dedicated herself to taking care of our Rambo.

During this time, I fondly remember his falling asleep on the floor next to me. (And I must admit I napped, too.) After resting for a while, we'd finally stand, and as we started to move, I would try to guide him away from running into the wall.

I was trying to protect him and keep him from hurting himself. But he would have nothing to do with that. He would pull as hard as he could and walk straight into the wall, no matter how firmly I tried to turn him.

Eventually, I would just let go, and he would walk until he hit the wall with his nose, stand there a few seconds, then turn and come with me.

I realized that he needed to get his bearings, or a sense of his surroundings, when he first stood, and the only way he knew how to do that was to first walk into the wall. Once he had his bearings, he could navigate through the house fairly well.

This was his routine, and I left him alone to find his own bearings after that.

His trust in me was truly unbelievable. I had another memorable experience with him one day when I took him for a walk after he had lost his vision. As usual, he was on his leash.

It was late fall and there was a cool, brisk wind in the air. This was about six months prior to Rambo leaving us, and he was rather frail by this time.

As we started down the street, I noticed that the cool air seemed to make him feel better, and he started nudging me with his nose. *Keep in mind, he was 100% blind!*

Well, he nudged me more and started to run down the street the way he often did when he was young, and we were on our morning runs together.

So, I started running with him, and he stayed close by my side, nudging me as we ran to keep finding his bearings. We ran all the way to the end of our street.

I was just amazed that he trusted me to make sure he wouldn't run into anything and that he let me guide him all the way to the end of our street with the wind in his hair and me by his side. *Sadly, it was our last run together.*

He was exhausted at the end of our run, and it took us twice as long to make it back to the house that evening. He lay down on the kitchen floor and fell fast asleep. After that, he never had the energy or the will to run or even go for a walk. It was as if he just wanted that one last run with 'Daddy' to experience the joy of it and to let me know he was still there for me.

I learned a great deal about life watching both Cooper and Rambo. I learned that even though Cooper was the dominant dog, Rambo was still his buddy, and they were quite a team.

I also learned that I needed to let Rambo find his own way. Only then would he let me help him and eventually follow me. He taught me that loyalty and trust are rare in life and must be earned.

I also learned that we should cherish the ones we love while we have the chance, because you never know when that 'Saturday morning' will come.

In real life, we all have lessons we've learned from someone -- our parents, our grandparents, and even our pets. As I look back on my time with my boys, I wish I had paid more attention to the lessons they were teaching me.

How often has someone tried to offer you advice or guidance about something, but you just *had* to do it your own way? Well, I've been guilty of that, too. Many times during my life, I *should have listened* to someone who wanted to teach me something or keep me from making mistakes.

The point I'm trying to make is that the lessons in this book are attempting to offer guidance and, hopefully, keep you from 'running into that wall' over and over again.

Like my Rambo, only you can decide if you're ready to trust someone to help you find your bearings and take that blind run with the wind in your face?

You never know where it might lead you?

6s = Cs

$$6S = CS$$

Chapter Nine
The CEO

(…who liked to hear himself talk.)

"Did you hear what I just said?"

We all know the old saying about God giving us two ears and one mouth for a reason … to listen twice as much as we talk.

In this story, I share a real experience I had with one CEO. But I believe it provides a good example of how some people, even those who are in positions of authority, like to hear themselves talk more than they like to listen to others. In turn, they make lots of mistakes.

As you progress through your career, regardless of your position, you'll benefit from the lessons in this story. I hope you'll remember them. Now on to the story.

During the consolidation era, I had just completed an assignment with one consolidator when I heard about another consolidator who was looking for a president to help run their newly acquired service and mechanical contracting businesses.

The company was struggling with how to organize these new businesses, and as described previously in this book, the existing owners, who stayed on under non-compete agreements, were disengaging and waiting for the new company to give them direction.

Since I like challenges, I decided to apply for the position. At least I could speak to them and learn more about what they were experiencing in the industry. After about a week, I received a call to go to one of their branch offices and talk about the position.

I drove ninety miles to their office and spent the day talking to both the branch president and the vice president. They asked many good questions about my background and what I thought I might be able to bring to their new venture.

I left the interview feeling pretty confident that I would be able to help this organization consolidate their branches and turn them around. I also thought I'd enjoy the position.

A few days later, I was asked to return for more interviews. So, I drove the ninety miles again and met with their HR manager, CFO, and several midlevel managers. They were all very pleasant, asked many good questions, and took the time to listen to my experiences and how I might be able to help them.

After nine separate interviews that day, I was also asked to take two computerized assessments designed to evaluate certain capabilities and determine my personality, with the results being compared to the position profile. Mind you, I have now been interviewed by eleven different people and taken two separate tests.

I really liked the thoroughness and detailed approach the organization was using to fill this position. After all, it was a key role within a new division of their company.

I drove home feeling pretty good about the situation and hopeful that they would offer me the position with the new business operation.

After waiting two days, I received another call. I was asked to go visit the actual companies that they wanted me to run. They invited me to spend the day talking with the CFOs and employees, having lunch with the previous owners (five total), and seeing if there was a good fit.

I drove another one hundred and twenty-five miles and spent the day at the facilities interfacing with the employees and the CFOs. I also had lunch with the previous owners.

After these meetings, I was convinced more than ever that I really liked this team. It felt like a good fit, and I saw the potential of my being able to help point this company in the right direction.

A week went by, and I was called again and given feedback that they really felt I was the one to take over their new operations. They now wanted me to visit their main headquarters and spend some time with their president /CEO.

So, I travelled to their headquarters and proceeded to the top floor (where else?) to meet with the CEO. I arrived on the top floor about fifteen minutes early and announced that I had an appointment with the president /CEO.

His executive assistant asked that I take a seat and said she would let him know I had arrived. Forty-five minutes passed, and I approached the executive assistant and asked if she knew how much longer I might have to wait. She checked and told me it wouldn't be long.

After waiting *another* forty-five minutes, I asked, again, how much longer it might be. By now,

I was thinking this might be some kind of pre-interview test the CEO liked to play on potential new employees. She checked, once again, and said it shouldn't be much longer.

Well, after waiting a total of two and a half hours, the CEO finally asked that I come in. I knew right then this didn't feel right. He never apologized for keeping me waiting, other than stating he was really busy. (I guess I didn't have anything better to do than sit around and wait to see him.)

At that point he started talking about "his" company, "his" employees, "his" plans for the future, "his" plans for the division I was interviewing to manage. He continued on and on for almost an hour and a half.

During this entire time, he didn't ask me a single question about my background, or my thoughts about what I had seen on my visit to their branch offices, or even if I would like something to drink (since I had been sitting in "his" lobby for over two hours). I did try to interject my thoughts into the conversation, but he just kept cutting me off time and again with,

"Did you hear what I just said?"

After talking continuously for such a long time, he finally ran out of things to say, told me he had another meeting, thanked me for coming in, and ushered me to the door.

As I walked to the parking lot, I asked myself, "What just happened?" This guy only focused on himself and had no clue about what was really needed to fix "his" new division. He just loved hearing himself talk, and talk, and talk. I think he believed *that* was his purpose in life as the CEO.

I decided right then and there that I did not want to work for such a person (since I would be answering directly to him if I took the position), so I called the branch president, with whom I first met, and advised him I was no longer interested in the position.

He was astonished by the news and asked why I had made such a decision. I described what had happened and explained that if the CEO was too busy to see me and only liked hearing his own voice, then he certainly wasn't going to have time to listen to anything I had to contribute.

To my surprise, the branch president commented that he felt the same way and that I wasn't the first to make that observation about their CEO. He apologized for taking so much of my time, expressed his regret that it didn't work out, and offered to be a reference for me if I ever needed one.

This experience is very similar to others I've had or heard about from colleagues throughout my career, which is a mark against our industry. Those in authority supposedly rise to the top because of their leadership skills, but I often wonder how some of them really get these positions of authority.

It's like finding '*turtles on a fence post'*. If they're on the fence post, it's always because *someone put them there*. They didn't get there on their own, and they probably don't belong there.

I wish the board of directors at larger corporations would complete a more thorough vetting process when searching and selecting talent for leadership positions. I also wish colleges would spend more time teaching real-world leadership skills in addition to business fundamentals.

The type of behavior demonstrated by the CEO in this story is not just limited to people in larger companies. Perhaps you were hired by a smaller company, or you achieved your position via 'start-up' or 'next generation,' or you married into the business. Regardless of how you got your position, please take note of this story and ask yourself,

"Do you talk more than you listen,
and are you guilty of these same actions?"

If you are, please try to change your behavior before you start implementing my six-step program into your organization or you are certain to fail. (And you'll lose some good people along the way.)

"Did you hear what I just said?"

An observation I made during this experience was that the employees of this firm were all working really hard to succeed, but they could have benefited from working smarter, not just harder.

We've all heard and used this expression many times. We know what it means and can relate to the sentiment. But frankly, I think we could add to the message. How about, "Let's enjoy life more, work hard *and* smart and always remember to give back to our industry?" OK, I know it sounds a little strange, but hear me out.

We can't help but get smarter when we give back to our industry and interact more with our peers. There's always something we can learn from them that will help improve our work and lives, and you'll get this result by *listening* more than talking.

I remember going to a seminar once and feeling so bored because the message was the same as I had heard a dozen times before. (I'll bet money you've been to the same seminars?)

As I sat there, I was thinking I could be getting work done in the office instead listening to some speaker deliver a message he'd obviously delivered a few hundred times before.

I honestly believed that the speaker, too, was thinking how he would love to be anywhere but there, and then it dawned on me to just interrupt at the right time and ask the question,

"Does this stuff really work?"

I remember this got the attention of the other attendees, and the speaker was a little stunned. The point I'm trying to make is, don't just sit there. If you're professional in your approach and wait for the right opportunity to ask your questions, I'm certain you'll be happy with the answers or responses you get in return. *Ask, then listen - what a novel idea.*

If you take time from your busy schedule to try to learn something new, make sure you do. Think about what the speaker is trying to teach, and then consider how you might apply it. If it doesn't make sense, ask for clarification, and listen to the response. I'll bet a dozen other people in the room probably have the same questions as you, but won't speak up because someone might think their 'dumb' questions.

I attended meetings early on in my career with owners and general contractors to learn about the construction sequence they were proposing, and I often thought to myself -- *that won't work for the mechanical contractor.* Yet, I continued to just sit there and say nothing. Why?

I said nothing because I was concerned that I might upset the general contractor, and I was also worried that they would think I had a dumb suggestion. **Who cares? Be smarter!** Please learn to speak up (in a professional manner) and ask questions or make suggestions without the fear of being judged. Isn't that what we learned to do in the first grade?

By asking and listening, you're learning, and by learning you're educating yourself. Give back to the industry through open discussions with your peers. Through these exchanges, everyone will learn to think differently and to see situations, issues, and solutions from different perspectives. This supports being smarter and not having to work harder. Don't be like the CEO in this story.

*Let's face it, we're contractors, and we are always going to work hard, so why not also get smarter along the way, and enjoy the ride just for the fun of it! – **Did you "listen" to what I just said?***

6S = CS

$$6s = Cs$$

Chapter Ten
The Contracting Business

Are you in the Contracting Business or is the Contracting Business in you?

If you're in the contracting business, but it's not in you, which means you're working in an industry that doesn't really excite you and to which you may not be fully committed, then you're just another contractor trying to make it in the business world.

However, if you're fully committed to and enjoy working in this industry more than any other, then the contracting business is *in* you, and you're most likely the type of business person that everyone else would like to be.

Let me explain . . .

Throughout my career, I've seen many very nice people in the contracting business working hard *trying to make it* in this competitive world, and I've seen a few very nice people working hard to make it, but also truly *enjoying* the business they were in.

You probably see yourself in one of these two groups, or perhaps somewhere between the two. But regardless of where you place yourself, you still want to succeed.

To make it in this business, you must be willing to *do your homework* if you expect to *pass the test.*

If you don't do your homework, you most definitely will never reach the level of success you desire, even though you love the business.

Let me ask you some basic questions, and let's see if you've - *done your homework:*

1) Did you prepare a five-year business plan prior to opening your doors?

2) Did you study your competitors and determine their markets, along with their strengths and weaknesses?

3) Did you research and really study your market to determine its size, what portion of it you currently had, what portion you wanted to capture, and how you would do it?

4) Did you prepare a list of your strengths, weaknesses, opportunities, and threats (SWOT analysis)? Using this information, did you determine your best market for delivering the quality products and services that would *differentiate* you from your competitors?

5) Did you prepare a one-year marketing plan, specifying what media to use and how much you would spend to brand your company in the business world? (Did you consult with a professional marketing company?)

6) Did you prepare a detailed budget that included all your expected costs? (Do you truly understand accounting; e.g., direct costs, gross margin, variable costs, fixed costs, total overhead, etc?)

7) Did you, did you, did you…….

The list can go on and on (and on!!), but the point you must remember is, unless you prepare to win, you're preparing to fail. *(Sorry for the cliché, but it's appropriate.)*

Many business owners join professional associations to learn industry best practices, but they have little to show for their time and money except, perhaps, a trip to Las Vegas (or another destination) where they spent long days sitting in a room with someone preaching at them on how to be a great leader or how to hire the best people. In my opinion, unless you've planned your schedule and thought about what you want to get from the sessions, you'll waste valuable conference time (and lots of money) just randomly attending seminars.

Please don't get me wrong. I really believe that most sessions or seminars can be extremely useful, as long as you attend with an open mind, actively participate in the experience, and are willing to learn something new.

Often however, what you *really* want to hear and learn more about is how successful companies or individuals make it, and how do they sustain their success year after year.

While reading many of the reviews of association conferences and meetings, I've noticed that members often comment that, for them, their best experiences were the roundtable discussions. They felt they learned more from these discussions than from the presentations.

Perhaps we appreciate the roundtable discussions because we're looking for people in the business who can relate to our experiences and situations. We can talk to them honestly about what's going on in our businesses, without being criticized or judged, and we feel they can help us by offering suggestions to guide us through the maze.

We're all looking for that edge that allows us to be successful, while not having to work so hard, day after day, with little or no results.

Has anyone ever suggested you sell your business to make a lot of money? Maybe you have been thinking about it lately. It's very tempting.

But, be cautious if and when considering this action. Don't sell your business thinking that if you make some money, you'll feel successful, because later you might wish you hadn't.

I can only say that I've met many business owners who were miserable after selling their companies because most (not all) entrepreneurs cannot give up their autonomy and work for another person, regardless of how much they think they can.

My advice is to think long and hard before making a decision to sell your business and talk to others who have previously sold their contracting companies. Make sure it's the right decision for you personally. *Get your counsel from diverse sources.*

Don't look for the easy way to success, because there isn't one!

Join an organization that will benefit you and that will allow you to contribute. Ask the hard questions about what determines success. Discuss ideas and experiences, and make sure you listen!

Help form business groups that can meet and share ideas. Why not start your own peer group by calling firms that are successful in different markets and seeing if they would like to meet periodically, exchange ideas, and share best practices? In my experience, these groups can be really beneficial to you and your business.

Whether you're new to the contracting PHVACR business or experienced, if you really want to succeed, put in the time to do the homework, and I'm confident that you'll pass the competition *so-o-o fast*, they won't know what hit them.

Remember, successful firms never stop looking for ways to improve.

6S = CS

6s = Cs

Chapter Eleven
Productivity

Improve Your Productivity.......Why?

Easier said than done, right? Why should I?

Everyone talks about improving productivity, but to actually do it is another story. *(Please read this chapter twice. It's that important!)*

I've had many occasions during my career to improve productivity using various means, and I've discovered some basic things you must know before you attempt it.

Make sure you understand the definition of what productivity really is.

Please look it up first thing tomorrow morning, write it down, then put it in a place where you'll see it every day.

This is a special request. Please listen to me, and you won't regret it!

There are dozens of courses and seminars you can take on productivity, and they are all useful. But we're contractors, and we like to get things done our own way and with as little outside interference as possible, right? Well, keep reading, and hopefully, you'll be able to get started.

Please try to understand the impact of improving productivity before you make any changes to your business.

At the beginning of this section, I asked why anyone should try to improve productivity? For many years, we've been taught that improving productivity 1% will increase your bottom line by *approximately* (please don't send me letters correcting me to the 10th degree – I said approximately) *26.5%+/-! That's why!*

This means if you can get all of your employees to improve their time by approximately (no letters now!) 24 minutes or 1% of one 40-hour week, you will essentially improve the percentage of your current EBIT or NIBIT by 26.5%+/-!

For example: If your current EBIT is 2.5%, your new EBIT would be 2.5% X 1.265, which is *3.1625% or a 26.5% improvement* to your bottom line. (Again, these are approximate numbers, so please, no letters!)

Now that's worth looking into as soon as you can! To get started, consider taking some of the following actions:

1) Brainstorm with your employees on how your team can improve productivity by first explaining to them the benefits and what it means to them (what's in it for them) and the company.

   You should be able to figure this one out without my help. I'll bet your team will come up with some great ideas that can get you started almost immediately. Offer them an incentive to attend the meeting and provide at least one great idea.

   Remind your team that the intent is to improve the time it takes to perform certain tasks and processes from beginning to end, *without jeopardizing quality*. Some examples to consider include: loading and stocking the trucks, adjusting the route to the site, handling material, installation procedures, clean-up, record keeping and document handling, equipment and tool availability, safety practices, etc. Get the idea?

The improvements may be large or small, but you're only asking your employees to improve their productivity *by a minimum of* *24 minutes a week, or 4.8 minutes* ***per day*** *per employee.*

Chart or diagram your current workflow, then look for ways to improve or shorten the timeline while improving quality and safety. *Doing this will help you improve three things at the same time.*

2) *Remember – You can't save time!! I repeat - no matter how much you improve productivity, you can't save time*. Make sure you have a plan to *utilize* the time you just inherited to continue to improve the next job and so on.

3) Don't just say: "Great. I improved my productivity, and now I'll sit back and wait for my extra 26.5%. It's not going to happen that automatically.

Monitor your improvements and provide your teams with timely feedback. If you're not going to establish a way to monitor your improvements and give feedback to your team, then don't even attempt to improve. Remember – *processes that are monitored or measured are more likely to improve.*

4) Set up a monthly meeting with your team to give and receive feedback on how their ideas are working, and solicit suggestions for other improvements.

5) Implement a job profit-sharing plan with your employees, and this will take off like a rocket!

   (Don't be stingy – I said share!!!)

Several things will happen if you ***at least try*** to improve productivity

- You'll have a better understanding of your business and how it works.

  That's a good thing right there!

- You'll show your employees how much you appreciate their knowledge and experience by including them in the decision-making process.

  One of the major reasons employees leave firms is that they feel underappreciated. So now we've added employee retention to the benefits of improving productivity.

That's another great plus!

You'll develop new methods to track labor and new operations that improve your productivity along with quality, safety, and your bottom line. *Try arguing with that!*

- With improved productivity, your current employees won't need to work as hard, and they will be able to enjoy life a little more. *Sounds like a win-win!*

- Another great result is you'll now be able to accept work you previously had to turn down because you couldn't meet the schedule and/or didn't have the manpower.

One of the most significant improvements you'll see is an increase in both your new customer and existing customer retention numbers. Acquiring and retaining customers creates job security for your employees. *Now we're really getting somewhere!*

Finally, I have a really *BIG* surprise for you. I've held off telling you until the end, because I knew you would get so excited you wouldn't be able to finish this section of the book!

My experience when implementing this plan has shown that although you start by focusing on a 1% improvement, you'll end up with *at least 5%!*

That equates to (Are you ready for this?)
a 65%+/- improvement in your EBIT percentage.

That means if you're willing to *"do your homework"* and put in the time and effort to identify possible changes and actually implement them, you just might end up with an improvement to your bottom line of 26.5% to 65% (minimum) without adding revenue or additional manpower!

Improve your productivity, and improve your bottom line!

You'll also improve morale, employee retention, safety, and customer retention; and you'll increase top-line revenue by allowing your firm to obtain more work with the same number of employees.

Now, do yourself a favor – consider reading this chapter again!

6S = CS

Chapter Twelve
The Balloon Ride

Is your balloon full of hot air? . . .or are you?

When I lived in an area where hot-air balloons were often visible, I decided to treat some visiting family members and my lovely wife to our very first balloon ride, so we could experience the thrill firsthand.

We arrived at the designated location, and the pilot came over and introduced himself something like this. "Hi. My name is Captain Bob, and I'll be your pilot today."

"Your regular pilot couldn't make it, so he asked that I step in. But don't worry. I have plenty of experience flying hot-air balloons. I've flown with the regular pilot many times."

He then looked us square in the eye and said, "The only problem is, although I've taken off many times, I've never had the opportunity to land one!"

My family and I just looked at him with our mouths open, not knowing how to respond or what to say. Before we could close our mouths, he said:

"I'm just kidding. Of course I know how to land a balloon. I did it once, a long time ago."

He was 'kidding' with us *again*. But despite his sense of humor, the pilot did a great job, and the flight turned out to be a wonderful experience. Best of all -- our landing was perfect!

The point of sharing this experience is to encourage you to consider the following question:

When you show up for work every morning, do you know how to run or 'pilot' your business effectively, so it doesn't 'fall to the earth' and crash?

Our pilot stopped on his way to the launch field and released a trial balloon to test the direction of the wind and its speed prior to our takeoff.

Although hot-air balloonists can't totally control their direction or speed when flying, they do have some idea of the direction in which they will be going when they launch the balloon.

Each morning when you arrive at work, are you aware and confident of your company's direction?

Before I leave work every day, I review what I didn't finish and make a list of what I plan to accomplish the next day.

I then prioritize the listed items, so when I show up at my office (or launch field) the following day, at least I know in what direction I should be heading.

As I've addressed in prior stories, if you don't have a plan or map for where you're going, you probably won't get there. If you're lucky enough to *stumble* to where you need to be, you'll soon realize that the path wasn't as direct as it could have been and the journey probably took longer than necessary, had you used a map (or business plan).

To be like our pilot friend, we should use the following procedures each morning to ensure our balloon is full of hot air and to know approximately in what direction we are going:

1. *Know the direction and speed of the wind before you leave the office each day.* Make a list and prioritize what you want to accomplish the next morning.

2. *Make sure you have enough tanks of propane to sustain the trip – or risk falling from the sky like a rock.* Make sure your employees have the tools to do the jobs you're expecting them to do that day, as well as the safety equipment and training to do them right.

3. *Have some idea of where you plan to land at the end of your trip, so your chase vehicle*

and crew can find you and help reload your balloon into the van. Then both you and your passengers can return home safely.

If you know each morning what you want to accomplish by the end of the day, you can schedule your time to achieve most, if not all, of these things.

By having a plan you'll finish the day (*your flight*) at approximately where you want and need to be. You won't be miles off course with nothing completed.

4. *Celebrate the successful flight with a traditional champagne toast.* Acknowledge your successes. Take the time to get your staff together whenever you have an opportunity to celebrate a victory, and share the win. Because you involved them, they'll know you see them as valuable team members.

The bottom line is:
Preplan everything. Overlook nothing.

If you do, you'll soon be celebrating both a successful flight and a great landing.

Have a great flight!

$$6S = CS$$

$$6s = Cs$$

Chapter Thirteen
CEO to Bill

"Don't come back to my office until you have a plan to show me how you're going to make up the losses!"

You'll love this story….

I remember being excited when I started with a large mechanical contracting firm as a senior project manager during my early days in the business. On my first day of work, I attended an orientation and received the *Project Managers' Manual*, which was about four inches thick. This manual was supposed to provide me with all the information I needed to work at the company.

When I returned to my office after the orientation, I opened the manual and started to read. I had only finished reading about two chapters, when my boss came to my office and 'dumped' about ten jobs on me. He told me that all the jobs were currently under construction and at least three months behind schedule. (*Sound familiar*?)

When I asked if I needed to know more about the company processes or the background on any of the jobs, I was told to just go out and do what I knew how to do, and the rest would come over time.

So, I went out into this strange new world and began to get on top of these projects to the best of my abilities, and for the first three months, I felt pretty good about what I was accomplishing.

This company (pre-computers) had a very defined process for setting up 'job folders' to capture and organize all the job-specific records such as bid documents, purchase orders, subcontracts, change orders, and general contractor (GC) contracts.

The 'job folder' also included a spreadsheet that showed material and labor breakdown codes for the entire job. We used the spreadsheets to track costs and update the projected gross margin quarterly.

The thing was - this company booked all jobs at the same gross margin, regardless of the bid number, and the project manager was expected to 'bring it in' at that number or else. Talk about pressure!

While at this company, I remember the CEO coming into my office many times and telling me he had good news and bad news. The good news was he had just come from a GC's office where he had negotiated and finalized contracts for several new jobs that I had bid earlier (maybe as much as several months). The bad news was he took them for cost!

Remember, this company required all jobs to be booked at the minimum required gross margin, regardless of the contract amount.

Well, by the end of the first quarter, I was managing twenty-three jobs, which meant I had twenty-three 'job folders' to prepare for review by the company's CEO. Overall, my jobs weren't too bad, and the average of all the jobs was above the minimum gross margin mandated by the company.

The day that the CEO was to meet with me for his first quarterly review of all my jobs finally arrived. I was nervous, as you might expect. But I was also confident that he would believe I was doing a great job, since I was carrying such a large workload and delivering respectable gross margin numbers.

Man, was I wrong! And to make matters worse, none of the other project managers had prepared me for what was about to happen.

I was invited into the CEO's rather oversized office. (I think it was large to intimidate visitors – and it worked!) He greeted me as I placed my twenty-three 'job folders' on his very imposing desk.

He asked me which job I wanted to review first, and I picked one that was fairly respectable, but not my best, thinking I would save the best for last - right?

This was the wrong decision!

The first thing he did was open the folder. He then unfolded this rather long spreadsheet that showed all the job's cost codes and the total projected gross margin at the bottom, including all the approved and outstanding change orders.

The bottom-line gross margin was 5% less than the minimum we were asked to maintain on all the jobs, because both the underground and first floor rough-in had gone over the budget. Both had been completed prior to my coming on board.

Well, what happened next changed my view on how to manage projects for the rest of my career.

He looked at the (lower than mandated) gross margin figure shown on the spreadsheet, then at the entire list of job cost codes with their projections, and then it happened.

His face got extremely red, the blood vessels in his neck turned bright blue, and his chest puffed up like a turkey ready to go into battle.

He looked at me with his piercing eyes, stood up, grabbed the open folder, and threw it as hard as he could against the wall of his office.

Now keep in mind that these folders only had those metal folding tabs holding everything in place.

When the folder crashed into the wall near the ceiling, the tabs opened, and the papers scattered everywhere. As I sat there in utter shock over what was happening, he leaned over the desk, put his finger in my face, and said something like:

"Get out of my office, and don't come back until you have a plan that shows me how you are going to make sure this job and all other jobs you're running will meet the minimum gross margin you're required to make. Your first and foremost job as a project manager is ***to make money***!"

As I was on the floor gathering all the papers that were falling down like small parachutes, I tried to recover from the shock and get my emotions under control. I just kept saying: "Yes sir, yes sir, I'm sorry. I didn't completely understand what you wanted."

At that point he told me the information was in the *Project Managers' Manual*, which I should have already read!

As I left his office with my arms full of the twenty-three folders and all the loose papers that I had just spent five minutes picking up off the floor, I noticed the other project managers standing around, waiting for their turn, and laughing their heads off.

It seemed that this was the CEO's normal practice for initiating new project managers, and all the others were just waiting to see my reaction. At the time, I didn't think it was funny. In fact, I was ready to just call it quits and go home. How could anyone work with a man like that?

Well, I went back to my office, recomposed myself, and thought about what had happened. This guy was pushing me to do better-than-average work.

I didn't like how the CEO treated me, but he really made an impact. I was wrong to just accept the fact that this job, as well as a few others assigned to me, had lost money and gone over on labor hours early in their construction schedules. And I was wrong when I didn't even *try* to recover the losses. Wow, what a great idea - ***Find a way to recover early losses!***

I had been fully prepared to just move on and try to meet the labor projections on each of the remaining labor codes. This was a reasonable, but average, approach, and I realized I could do better.

I went back to the jobsite and met with the foreman. Together we reviewed the upcoming labor tasks and actually put together a plan to recover the lost hours and get the project back on schedule.

I always took pride in my work. I learned to be more resilient and to never let daily failures derail the ultimate success of my projects. This relentless push to succeed by paying attention to all the details is a very useful lesson that can be passed on to others.

I learned to work closely with my team. If needed, I didn't hesitate to bring in other project managers and foremen to the jobsites or office to help find ways to overcome any losses, and this became the norm on all projects. Taking advantage of the ideas and ingenuity of all available resources was an approach I used at this and other companies for the rest of my career.

I remember this same CEO once telling me that if two people want to work together, the details will pull them together. But if they don't want to work together, the details will push them apart.

This may sound a little deep, but it's really not. The message is this. When trying to accomplish something in life, whether it's a deal or just trying to resolve a conflict, first find common ground, then find the details you can agree upon. If everyone involved truly wants to find a resolution and work together, they will – and the rest will fall into place.

If they don't, walk away.

A final note…Please don't react the way the CEO did in this story. People don't always understand how you might want things done, even if you give them a four-inch-thick book of instructions.

Hire capable employees, give them what they need to do their work, explain the expectations, and move forward. Then, let them have some room to explore new ideas while they become accustomed to the new company.

Try to keep an open mind,
and, by all means, never micromanage them.

6S = CS

$$6S = CS$$

Chapter Fourteen
The Boat

Never name your boat <u>Bad Luck</u>!

As I mentioned earlier in the book, I lived in southern California before moving to Indiana in my early teens, and I worked in my dad's auto garage/junkyard with my older brother, Ray.

Sometimes, my dad worked on cars even when he knew the owners didn't have the money to pay him. In these cases, he agreed to a trade of some kind as payment for his work.

One time, he replaced an engine in a customer's car, and in return, the customer gave him a homemade, 18½ foot wooden cabin cruiser boat with an inboard engine. Needless to say, we were all excited to have a boat and looked forward to taking her out on the ocean.

The first time we took the boat out from Pierpoint Landing in Long Beach, the engine died in the middle of the bay, and we had to be towed back to shore. That's the day my dad named the boat *Bad Luck,* and - believe me - it lived up to its name!

I could share many, many stories of our adventures on the open sea, but I'm going to share the one about the incident that most affected me and taught me a lesson I have never forgotten.

My dad had planned for my brother and me to go fishing with him on Saturday morning. So, after closing the garage on Friday, we started to prep the boat for our deep-sea-fishing adventure the next day. Everyone had a chore to do to get the boat ready. My brother made sure the boat had gas in the tank, and my dad made sure all the gear was on board and stored properly, the trailer tires had the proper pressure, and the brake lights worked. I was the youngest (ten years old), so I was assigned to do whatever was left.

As my dad inspected our wooden trailer and the blocks that the boat sat on, he noticed that both of the top blocks were loose and not secured to the bottom ones. He told me to go to the work bench, get some nails, and nail the blocks back together. *Big mistake!*

I found the hammer and some nails and really did a good job nailing them together nice and tight, so my dad would be proud of me. (Don't get ahead of the story yet!).

He checked my work and told me I had done a good job. My dad rarely gave compliments, so his praise made me feel really good.

The next morning, we all got up before dawn and drove the trailer and boat down to Pierpoint Landing, so the guy with the overhead crane could put the straps under the boat and lift her up and into the water.

We were all really excited, since we hadn't taken the boat out recently. While my dad was inside paying the bill, the crane operator lowered the slings down, and my brother and I slipped them under the boat. We then backed away, so the operator could lift the boat and put it into the water.

As my brother and I stood there watching the operator lift the boat, we noticed something strange and unexpected start to happen. Both the boat and the trailer were being lifted at the same time.

They were raised about fifteen feet in the air when my dad came out of the shanty and noticed what was happening. He looked at my brother and me and instantly yelled, "What did you do?"

I couldn't understand how this could be our fault? After all, we weren't the ones lifting the boat.

It was at this point that we all started to hear a loud cracking sound. Then, we heard a very loud pop. The bottom of the boat broke away, and the trailer, which had a large portion of the boat's hull attached to it, came crashing to the ground!

Wow! What a sight to behold.

At that point, I just thought the crane operator was about to feel the wrath of my dad for destroying our one and only boat, the *Bad Luck.*

Boy was I wrong! My dad ran over to the trailer while it was still bouncing off the pavement and stood there staring at the hull of our boat, trying to figure out why chunks of it were still fastened to the trailer.

Ok – so you've probably figured it out already, but please let me finish my story.

He immediately noticed that nails were sticking up from the trailer supports on both sides, all the way up through the chunks of the hull of the boat.

Keep in mind these weren't just your ordinary, run-of-the-mill nails. I wanted to do a good job and make my dad proud of me, so I used the best nails I could find. If I remember correctly, I think I used 20-penny nails. Oh yah, the really big ones!

Of course, the boat was still hanging in the air, just blowing in the wind, but this time the wind was blowing through two gigantic holes on either side of the hull.

Well, what happened next is still a bit fuzzy, but I'll try to paint the picture as best as I can.

My dad's face turned bright purple, and the blood vessels in his face were sticking out. I'm certain the blood vessels on his neck would have been sticking out, too, that is - if he had a neck. My dad was around 6' tall and weighed over 375 lbs., and he didn't have much neck that I can recall seeing. However, I do remember that, for a man his size, he was really fast!

Picture my dad chasing a five-foot, 100 lb., ten-year-old boy around the dock, with our trailer and boat sitting in shambles in the middle of the boatyard in Long Beach, on a sunny Saturday morning.

I started to run, and my dad chased after me. (I was sure he wanted to kill me!) Then, three dock workers chased after my dad to try to stop him, and my brother ran behind all of them, just because he wanted to join in the fun of seeing my dad kill his younger brother, which he had been wanting to do for years. (But my dad wouldn't let him.)

It was like a scene from an old Keystone Cops movie. Got the picture?

Now, throw into the mix a lot of profanity similar to what was heard in the scene from the **Christmas Story** movie when the furnace exploded, and you have the picture in your mind of my Saturday morning fishing trip, just as I remember it after all these years.

Needless to say, my dad ran out of steam, and the chase ended. But our trip home was not pleasant (definitely not part of the story I want to share). The yelling of profanity didn't stop for what seemed like a month. Of course, I was grounded, and my dad made me fix the boat.

That was the summer I learned how to apply fiberglass layers to a boat hull and, afterwards, how to soak my hands and arms every evening to try to relieve the itching caused by the fiberglass. However, the repair made the boat hull better than the original, and we did get in a few more fishing trips. And as you know, my dad didn't kill me, much to the dismay of my older brother.

One positive outcome for me –
I never again had to help get the boat ready!

Now for the lessons. As I've always said, when you want someone to do something for you, be sure to always give clear directions.

Don't presume they know what you expect. Have them paraphrase back to you what they heard you say, just to make sure they understand not to use 20-penny nails where they are not needed.

Secondly, make sure you give the instructions to someone who can get the job done. In other words, make sure they have received the proper training in the first place.

Also, don't presume they are the right person for the job. They just might be that proverbial *turtle on a fence post*.

And the final lesson is to never, ever name your boat, or anything else, *Bad Luck.*

Try to develop a positive attitude whenever you face problems. People around you will sense and be influenced by your energy. If we all commit to maintaining a positive outlook, our industry will improve, and we will create greater opportunities to have a successful and rewarding career.

6s = Cs

Chapter Fifteen
Helpful Hints

- Join a peer group.
- Join an industry organization *and* participate.
- Enjoy being with your family whenever you can.
- Love what you do.
- Learn to forgive others.
- Always have faith in yourself.
- Get up when you're knocked down.
- Get up again and keep moving forward.
- Take time for yourself.
- Take time for your family.
- Show your employees that you appreciate them.

- Pass this book on to a friend (or ask them to get one or two copies of their own).
- Enjoy life.
- Give back to our industry.
- Work hard, but be smart about it.
- Train your employees for the future.
- Take a class.
- Teach a class.
- Read another book.
- Write a book.
- Be proud of your accomplishments.
- Be proud of your company.
- Know your business inside and out.
- Pay attention to the details.
- Don't micromanage your employees.
- Know your business numbers.
- Know your competition.

- Get to know your employees.
- Write a mission and vision statement.
- Share your vision.
- Write a strategic plan.
- Work with an office employee for a day.
- Work in the field for a week.
- Listen twice as much as you talk.
- Provide constructive feedback.
- Be your company's cheerleader.
- Do what needs to be done, and make the tough decisions when necessary.
- Understand how to manage the change process.
- Understand the impact of productivity.
- Understand revenue growth vs. increase in productivity.
- Take a *new tack* when necessary.
- Learn to *sail* your business smoothly.

- Look to the future while taking care of the present.
- Write a business/marketing plan.
- Reinvent your company
- Reenergize your company.
- Reenergize yourself.
- Reenergize your management team.
- Take a vacation with your family.
- Splurge on yourself at least once.
- Continue to believe in yourself.
- Continue to believe in your team.
- Sell the ranch, not the chickens.
- Get your *turtles off the fence posts*.
- Give clear instructions to the right person.
- Each day, know the direction of the path your company is taking.

- Go for a walk (or run) with your dog.
- Don't be the frog who just *decides* to jump off the log. Go ahead and make the leap of faith.
- Don't *think you know* what to do to succeed with your business, make sure you *know* what to do.
- Find balance between work and your home life.
- Never use 20-penny nails when regular ones will do.
- Never name your boat *Bad Luck.*
- Accept the hard questions without feeling threatened or intimated.

If this book has taught you anything, please pass it on to a friend so they, too, can have an opportunity to learn and grow and to apply my six-step program to their businesses.

You, too, can *Make a Difference…*

This is not the end….

It's a –

"New Beginning"

Remember:
6s = Cs
(Qp + Qp + Es)

Six Steps = Contracting Success
(or any other business)

Thank you, again, for allowing me into your company.

Best of Luck...Bill

www.ingramcontent.com/pod-product-compliance
Lightning Source LLC
Chambersburg PA
CBHW030927180526
45163CB00002B/485
9781523730704